Before I Was a Critic I Was a Human Being

BEFORE I WAS A CRITIC
I WAS A HUMAN BEING

AMY FUNG

BOOK*HUG PRESS TORONTO
ARTSPEAK VANCOUVER
ESSAIS NO. 7
2019

The production of this book was made possible through the generous
assistance of the Canada Council for the Arts and the Ontario Arts Council.
Book*hug Press also acknowledges the support of the Government of Canada
through the Canada Book Fund and the Government of Ontario through the
Ontario Book Publishing Tax Credit and the Ontario Book Fund.
    This is one of the 200 exceptional projects funded through the Canada Council
for the Arts' New Chapter program. With this $35M investment, the Council
supports the creation and sharing of the arts in communities across Canada.

Book*hug Press acknowledges the land on which it operates. For thousands
of years it has been the traditional land of the Huron-Wendat, the Seneca, and
most recently, the Mississaugas of the Credit River. Today, this meeting place is
still the home to many Indigenous people from across Turtle Island, and we are
grateful to have the opportunity to work on this land.
    Artspeak acknowledges that is located on the unceded territories of the
xwməθkwəẏəm (Musqueam), Skwxwú7mesh (Squamish) and Səl̓ílwətaʔ
(Tsleil-Waututh) First Nations.

LIBRARY AND ARCHIVES CANADA CATALOGUING IN PUBLICATION

Title: Before I was a critic I was a human being / Amy Fung.
Names: Fung, Amy, author. | Artspeak Gallery, issuing body.
Series: Essais (Toronto, Ont.) ; no. 7.
Description: First edition. | Series statement: Essais series ; no. 7
Identifiers: Canadiana (print) 20190082690 | Canadiana (ebook) 20190082828

ISBN 9781771665056 (softcover)
ISBN 9781771665063 (HTML)
ISBN 9781771665070 (PDF)
ISBN 9781771665087 (Kindle)

Classification: LCC PS8611.U64 B44 2019 | DDC C814/.6—dc23

PRINTED IN CANADA

Contents

Nation-states are configurations of origins as exclusionary power structures which have legitimacy based solely on conquest and acquisition. Here at home in Canada, we are all implicated in this sense of origin.

—DIONNE BRAND

Perhaps it is the role of art to put us in complicity with things as they happen.

—LYN HEJINIAN

When I ask someone where they're from nowadays I expect a very long answer.

—STUART HALL

Prologue

I was last notably called a "chink" in 2011 while living in Scotland, that land and people who still fancied calling Indian restaurants "pakis" and Chinese restaurants "chinkies." I was cutting through a schoolyard when a young boy called over in my direction about what a chink I was. His mom stood nearby, waiting to pick him up and watching in silence. I was stunned, but not because a small Scottish child was throwing slurs at me or that his parental figure did nothing. I was shocked and confused because I spoke better English than he did, and that in my mind made me better than he would ever be.

Born in Hong Kong and raised in Canada, my mind has been a deeply colonized place.

While this lad showed me the prejudice in his heart, I wasn't exactly injured by his words. Neither he nor anyone in that town held any power over me. I was a visitor, parachuted in for a six-month arts writing residency under the guise of a diversity fellowship. I was an imported foreign good, put on display in the local museum during weekday hours as the visiting writer. I fielded frequent questions about whether I was actually Korean or Japanese. When I simply replied I was Canadian, no one ever followed up about where within Canada I had come from. They just politely smiled as if they already knew it was a place where I couldn't belong.

Perhaps in the context of a small town in the North East of Scotland, it was unbelievable to see a person of colour, at least one who wasn't working at one of two ethnic restaurants. I was being paid to review the goings-on of the town from my foreign perspective, complete with critiques, which has on more than one occasion led to the notion that I must be an "ungrateful bitch." Because how dare I try and critique the status quo, when I should just be thankful for being here.

The role of playing the foreigner, the Other, amongst a sea of Scottish people, was neither pleasant nor anything new to me. The main difference was that there was no myth of multiculturalism in Scotland, and when racism reared its egregious head, it never appeared in sheep's clothing.

I share this story as a way to demonstrate my thinking about language and power. I also understood Canada a lot better after living in Scotland. One of the central themes in this collection of stories is the violence of whiteness that is both around me and inside of me. Words alone can lift you up and throw you down, but I am more interested in thinking through who gets to speak and to whom are they speaking.

As another entry point, during a 2017 welcoming ceremony for Syrian refugees in Toronto, the officials gave a land acknowledgement and informed them that they were now settlers on this land. I would be later told how the translator could not find an appropriate Syrian word for *settler*, as the closest translation would be *Israeli*, who for generations have settled and occupied unceded Palestinian land.

I can't begin to assume the mental and emotional reception of those Syrian families and individuals who were told they have now become the Israelis of Canada. I can only point to the double-speak of the Canadian government's language. There is at once an admission that this land is inhabited by Indigenous Nations and, at the same time, still no official regard for Indigenous sovereignty on the land that so many of us have come to call home. It is akin to welcoming strangers in need into your neighbour's house, which you have pilfered and taken by force.

A core theme I revisit throughout this collection is how racialized immigration is perpetuating colonialism into the twenty-first century. I know the nation-state wants and depends on this continuation of internalized colonial entitlement, but what about the agency of new immigrant settlers? When I became a Canadian citizen in 1992, there was no land acknowledgement offered. Only in my thirties am I becoming aware of just some of the names of the hundreds of nations who live across these lands. I have mostly learned these names through the voices of Indigenous leaders and thinkers, scholars and activists, artists and writers, and more recently by settler politicians and bureaucrats. There is a lot of listening and unlearning that most settlers, newly immigrated or not, have to do in this generation and the ones still yet to come, and asking from a logistical point of view, how do we support Indigenous rights in this country without it being controlled and commodified by empire? I am aware I am writing in English and this is being read in English, that the production and research of this text was paid for by the Canada Council for the Arts, and that I hold citizenship to the nation of Canada. I am thankful for these opportunities, even if I am repeatedly told and shown how I don't really belong.

In my twenties, I distinctly remember the first time I used the phrase *Turtle Island*. I remember it well because I used it incorrectly and was immediately shamed by a white woman in Vancouver for not knowing how much land Turtle Island encompassed. She quickly and passive-aggressively suggested, in a sentence that lifted into a question, *I'm pretty sure Turtle Island covers all of North America?* I shrugged. I didn't know. I grew up in Edmonton, where I had never heard that phrase before 2010.

I didn't know the Anishinaabe creation story of Turtle Island back then, but neither did this white woman when I asked her where that name came from. This disconnection between information sharing and shaming has been typical, unhelpful, and continues on. As a first-generation settler, I began holding a lot of shame about not knowing Indigenous history and world views. I also hold a lot of privilege as an Asian woman with no accent other than a faint British enunciation. And yet, being shamed by the very same white Canadians who feel the need to create a diversity box and also lord their racial solidarity and Indigenous allyship over me is far more insulting than being called a chink by that small Scottish boy. The intention here is far more insidious through the hegemony of language and belonging.

PART II

As a product of the Canadian education system from 1988 through 2008, I was systematically taught nothing that would suggest Indigenous culture was anything but a historical chapter between the Hudson Bay Company's insatiable appetite for beaver pelts and the glory of the Loyalists during the War of 1812. Everything I learned I have had to unlearn. For example, when my family immigrated to Edmonton in the late 1980s, I would often see individual men, sometimes women, laid out on the sidewalks and front stoops across Chinatown. At first I couldn't tell what ethnicity they were. My only reference at that point, coming from Kowloon, was that they looked Filipino, but taller. I didn't understand the conflation of poverty with segregated ethnic neighbourhoods until decades later, but I ended up associating Indigenous identity with the brutal and indecipherable circumstances of street-level poverty for years to come.

Across Canada, Chinatowns were formed on the "other side" of the tracks due to another type of segregation, but as most of central Edmonton in the late eighties and nineties looked like it had formed on the "other side" of the tracks, it took longer for me to untangle the strands of homelessness, resource extraction, displacement, and the legacies of oppression in that boom-and-bust fort town.

By 1990, my family had moved into our third home in two years as my mother searched restlessly for a neighbourhood to call home. Living in older established neighbourhoods made her feel like an outsider, so we kept moving into newer and more distant subdivisions where everybody was a stranger to each other. In my new elementary school, new to me and new in the sense that the building had just been constructed, I remember first learning about Inuit culture during a special module on the topic of cultures in the far north. At the time, I actually couldn't imagine going any farther north than Edmonton. The entire class watched a video that I would see repeatedly over the years that showed an Inuk man cutting out large cubes of snow to assemble an igloo. Everyone would try and fail to create our own igloos during recess, eventually settling for cavernous holes instead. Every student was also given a piece of soapstone to sand down into our own version of a four-legged silhouette. After firing them in the kiln, we were told that carving and selling soapstone had become an important part of Inuit economy. We were not told why art had replaced hunting and trapping, but this was the first time anyone had conflated art-making and commerce to my young mind. This was a Grade 3 class, so I understand if there was no discussion of the forced relocation of Inuit communities by the federal government or how northern communities face the country's highest rates of youth suicide. We were taught that Inuit were a unique people and culture, living just north of us, and that it was no longer acceptable to call people by outdated language like *eskimo*, even if our city's football team thought otherwise.

The following year, my entire school was assembled into the gymnasium to watch *Dances with Wolves* on what was then still known as Aboriginal Day. I know we were not the only elementary school in the Prairies to offer this type of miseducation. It was the first time I watched this Oscar-winning movie, the first of many times, and I still remember that initial feeling of visceral and emotional manipulation when the music swelled and the camera panned to the dead wolf. As feature-film narration goes, all of the empathy centred on a white man's disillusionment with his own culture and subsequent appropriation of other people's traditions. Of course, it won Best Picture. While the teachers fast-forwarded through the sex scenes, it was business as usual for the entire elementary school as we sat through scenes of massacre and violence.

PART III

Leaving the Prairies, and after extensive and repeated travels coast to coast, the only thing authentically Canadian across all its distinct regions is the ugliness of the Canadian myth that Indigenous peoples, Black people, and people of colour, are somehow less than white settlers. Specifically, language used to denigrate Indigenous peoples was so common and varied that it was a lexicon unto its own. The same derogatory words that have been echoed to me for my entire lifetime in Canada, words that have been spoken to me by friends, neighbours, radio, television, newspaper articles, and editorials, and I never questioned any of it. I was caught off guard by these racist slurs when they appeared in KC Adams's *Cyborg Hybrid* portraits. I encountered this work for the first time in 2008 at the Banff Arts Centre. As I passed each photograph of a model wearing a white shirt with white text stitched across the front, I could hear the countless times someone uttered these stereotypes of Indigenous people to me, and how I never once challenged them. The series as a whole marked the first time I was visually confronted with contemporary Indigenous art outside of an anthropological and ethnographic setting, and by an artist of my generation.

In the region, important and often invisible figures like Marjorie Beaucage had already been doing the work of building systems of self-representation. Along with a group of people in the Edmonton region, Beaucage would relay years later how they took over an existing film festival that showed works about Indigenous culture and turned it into Dreamspeakers, a film festival for and by Indigenous people. This is an art history I am only learning decades later, and this knowledge still does not yet exist in the shape of textbooks or archives. It had taken twenty years of living in Canada before I came across Indigenous self-determination, and where political organizing was out of my purview then, art showed me how we see the world through individual subjectivities.

The majority of models in *Cyborg Hybrid* were also the faces of artists and curators leading contemporary Indigenous art to the forefront of national and international dialogues. People like Greg Hill and Candice Hopkins were building on the monumental work of curator Lee-

Ann Martin, and before her, artists Daphne Odjig, Alex Janvier, Jackson Beardy, Norval Morrisseau, and others as they successfully fought for the first contemporary Indigenous art exhibitions in this country in the late sixties and seventies.

From 2008 and on, I observed a rise in exhibitions featuring contemporary Indigenous artists in the Prairie region. After *Anthem* at the Walter Phillips Gallery, the next memorable show was *Face the Nation*, an exhibition at the newly rebranded Art Gallery of Alberta that brought together KC Adams, Dana Claxton, Maria Hupfield, Kent Monkman, Lori Blondeau, and others. At the opening, I remember seeing three of the women artists linked together, walking arm in arm, grinning ear to ear. I would ask Maria about this moment a decade later, and she remembered it, too, naming it the first time many of them had ever shown together.

But a few days after the opening at the AGA, I went back to see the exhibition without the crowds and witnessed a young Indigenous man trying to get into the show. Judging from his questions, he had never been to the gallery before and didn't know where to go. The front-desk attendant, an older white woman who had been at her seat for decades, gave him so much grief about his questions and his backpack that he turned around and left the building. She offered me a conspiring look of exasperation and relief, and I regret to say that I saw the show again that day and that young man did not. In that moment, I felt closer to whiteness than not. I was completely complicit and didn't think twice about entering a space that could cover its walls with images of contemporary Indigenous perspectives, but exclude their physical bodies from entering and experiencing. In that moment, I felt like a *real* Canadian.

During my first winter in Canada in 1988, I was then oblivious to the national protests being led by the Lubicon Lake Cree in northern Alberta against the *Spirit Sings* exhibition at the Glenbow Museum in Calgary. I would later hear about and see for myself how common it was to bring together artworks—including sacred objects—from across many nations, into a pan-Indigenous display of colonial gluttony. The exhibition has since been framed as a breaking point for how Indigenous cultures had been reduced to a museological study rather than living, breathing world views whose treaty rights were being ignored. Sponsored by the same oil and gas corporations that were actively destroying the Lubicons' way of life, the protests gained international attention and shamed Canada's hypocrisy in showcasing Indigenous culture as the central exhibition during the 1988 Winter Olympics while systematically harming their ongoing ways of life with aggressive and toxic methods of oil and gas extraction. While the show was contested from the start by numerous bands and nations, as well as prominent voices from the visual arts, academics, and allied activists, the Glenbow still benefited from high attendance numbers from national and international visitors in search of an authentic Canadian experience.

The Canadian experience cannot be removed from the Canadian imaginary, which, as a byproduct of culture being produced in this country, continues to serve and protect a white masculine settler-colonial hegemony. This series of chapters or short stories traces my movements across the predominantly southern half of this country we call Canada. I wrote from the position that I am seen, which is both visible and invisible, not white and almost white. Mostly, I am a silent observer, by choice and by default. From the beginning, I wanted to find the history and present-day relationship of racialized peoples to Indigenous nations, but I found only the controlling hand of colonialism as the central spectre in every narrative I came across. I then thought I could write the equivalent of an extremely long land acknowledgement that would encompass the moment I arrived to the moment that just passed. In examining my own life experiences, a perspective I still have not seen fully fleshed out in this country, I have been shaped through the bubble and the opportunity to analyze the country through a contemporary art lens. To defer to the words of Stuart Hall once more, "You have to go to art, you have to go to culture—to where people imagine, where they fantasize, where they symbolize"—to see how difference really operates inside each of our minds.

DISCLAIMER
The past lives on in the present. I have kept at the forefront of mind how these stories are going to be received by Indigenous and settler readers and thinkers, in and out of the art world, and under different rules of engagement in a time where call-out culture runs rampant. I have asked a multitude of readers to take a look, people I trust to hold me to task. It is still only my responsibility in the end if an error has been made, or a judgment call missed. In describing this project as a book about Canadian art and

identity, it has never been my intention to outline the impossible moniker of "Canadian art." This is *my* Canadian art, and even then, this claim is not an urgent possession.

In the process of writing this work of fictionalized nonfiction, I have changed and not changed a variety of proper nouns for many reasons, all of them personal and not meant to be shared. Seeking permissions, sharing countless drafts, incorporating feedback, and aware that people can still change their minds after publication, I have attempted to be as respectful as possible with stories that overlap with my own. I also haven't kept in touch with every single person who has informed my world view, and that is unfortunate, but sometimes very necessary. So, as fair warning, all likeness to any living persons in this book is through sheer coincidence. Even if you think something is about you, it likely is, but it's still not really about you.

For my mother

Harbour

you were either
Anglo
Franco
Black
Métis
Inuit
First
Nations
POC
Immigrant
if you happened to be more than
one of these
identities
did not fit into
one of these
identities
you defaulted into
one of these
identities
if you were lucky
you must be so lucky
to be here.

It's 1988, and a young man on television dabs at his eyes with a much-used tissue as camera flashes go off all around him. His hair looks slightly longer in the back than it does in the front. His voice trembles and cracks when he speaks about leaving the great city of Edmonton behind.

My mother, Cho Kei, just arrived in this city, so she has no idea what he's talking about. What's so great about this place? What's so great about this skinny boy? Having just moved her three daughters across the Pacific Ocean to a country where she knows no one, she does not see why anyone would cry over this dusty, empty city.

I cried a lot about Edmonton, but not for the same reasons as the "Great One." I was moved one month shy of completing first grade, and would have to complete Grade 1 twice—once in Kowloon and once in Edmonton. In the now-former colony of Kowloon, Hong Kong, British subjects were expected to speak, if not learn, some modicum of the Imperial language. Even after the handover back to China, the English language persists, along with a hybrid hijacking of both Cantonese and Mandarin—a pidgin that has risen to the status of an unofficial official language. Children queued up for the tram and always held the rail on the lift. They played football on a pitch and walked their dogs on leads; they ate their egg salad and watercress sandwiches on plates, not saucers, and carried umbrellas in their knapsacks.

I never could string any of these words together. Until I had to.

Cho Kei takes six-year-old me to one of her farewell lunches with her friends. While I am happily slurping up macaroni in consommé with thin strands of ham, my mother cajoles me into saying something in English. I act shy, because I am shy, or was shy, but after some prodding, I meekly whisper, "How are you?" The showmanship of this moment should have tipped me off that something was up. Cho Kei had never before asked any of her daughters to speak English, because she herself had never thought it necessary to speak English.

St. Mary's Elementary School in Kowloon was a doomful place, with a foreboding set of stairs leading up to a poorly lit hallway branching off into clinically depressive classrooms. The headmistress looked like a villain from every Hollywood movie Cho Kei had ever seen. She had taken me to see such foreign films as *King Kong*, *Snow White*, and *The Spy Who Loved Me*—all of which had sent me running out of the theatre, screaming in tears.

My mother knew I was an emotional child, but she would never have assumed the cruelty of white people would leave such a deep impression on me. Like her daughter, she preferred watching local films on the family TV, which, looking back, were almost always of the crude and lewd variety, starring Hong Kong superstars Chow Yun-Fat and Anita Mui Yim-fong. This early immersion in violent and ribald entertainment was not uncommon, and would become foundational to my visual repertoire, if not my gender identity. Choreographed violence, regurgitated Western pop music, and street food would be my everything.

My mother coddled me, and I loved it. St. Mary's employed

a heavy hand toward disciplinary behaviour, including a rule that parents were never allowed to walk their children past the front doors. We were expected to learn from an early age to do things on our own, starting with our morning climb up the steep and poorly lit stairwell. Beyond the skyscraper of stairs presided the even more foreboding figure of the headmistress, who stood there each morning, surveying her territory to ensure that no child would be helped. She never cracked even the slightest smile, and the white teachers were as skittish around her as the students, which, to my knowledge, consisted only of well-behaved Chinese boys and girls. From the very bottom of the stairs, my anxiety frequently led to tears. Each day, bless my mother, she would leave me at the door of the school, then race up to the terrace across the street so that by the time I sat down at my desk each morning I could see her waving at me from outside the classroom's second-storey window.

After school each day, beginning when her youngest was three, Cho Kei picked her up for their after-school snack together: a bowl of noodles or some macaroni and ham. I did my homework in the living room while she prepared dinner in the kitchen. In lieu of a family dog, Cho Kei liked taking her three daughters out for walks on the terrace when it was too hot to sit inside. If she was too tired, she would watch TV with her youngest while her teenage daughters did their homework in their shared room. Her husband left early in the morning and came back late in the evenings; dinners at home were always set for just four places in a family of five coexisting in a small two-bedroom apartment.

By the summer of 1988, Cho Kei moved her daughters across the Pacific into a much larger two-bedroom apartment just north of Jasper Avenue. Edmonton was the capital of a province named after Queen Victoria's fourth daughter, Princess Louise Caroline Alberta. Soon after settling into their downtown apartment, Cho Kei was disturbed by how silent it was all the time. The piercing scream of an ambulance, or the wailing echo of fire trucks, stretched wide across the horizon. There were not enough buildings or people to absorb such sounds. Vast stretches of parking lots separating one-storey buildings held zero resonance. She thought if she closed her eyes she could hear each grain of wind-born sand scratching against the concrete, sweeping into the cracks of broken asphalt. She had never watched a Western movie before moving to Alberta, and at the first sight of a lonely, noisy tumbleweed rolling through a forgotten town, Cho Kei's mouth and eyes broke open into laughter.

Eventually, as fall rolled around, Cho Kei moved her daughters into a house where everyone had their own bedrooms for the first time in their lives. I preferred to stay in her room, and the feeling was mutual. My mother walked me to Grade 1 every morning and picked me up again at the end of each day. She was there the first and second times that blood-spilled accidents unfolded on the playground. No one was to blame, but she blamed herself anyways.

Her husband didn't stay in Edmonton past two weeks, but that was the agreed-upon arrangement. He remained in Hong Kong to work and send money, and she would raise the children alone. They talked every few days, and her frustration with her husband always matched the decibel level she used to speak to him. She still went for walks in the evenings, when weather permitted, but finding a job, learning to drive, and sorting out her family's immigration papers, by herself, in a foreign language, were also part of the arrangement.

After switching schools and houses three times in the first three years, Cho Kei let all of her daughters find their own way to school through suburban shortcuts and empty fields. Her three daughters were speaking only English at home by this point, especially if friends were over or if they were on the phone. She was happy about this, but sad, too. After sending her eldest daughter off to college and starting a small business in the form of a fresh-flower shop, Cho Kei was finally doing something on her own. One weekend, she left on a business trip and didn't call in to check up on her two remaining children. She couldn't be reached where she was. I wasn't sure if she was coming back. She was no longer hiding or suppressing her anger and sadness at being in this country that was cold and not her own. When she did return, something had changed. She slammed chairs and threatened to leave for good. She didn't want to go back to Kowloon, but there was no clause to make her stay. She just stayed anyway.

Cho Kei and Hing Him bought their first apartment together in 1978, six years after they landed in Kowloon. They initially lived with his parents, but she did not get along with her mother-in-law, whose old ways of thinking had carried forward to their new lives. After two years, Cho Kei had had enough. She believed her mother-in-law resented her for her upbringing and class, which, in the old ways, would have been ranked higher than that of her in-laws. For this difference, or any difference, there would always be a price to pay. Cho Kei's family hailed from Beijing, and Hing Him was always so proud that his wife spoke Beijing Mandarin, which was understood to be the equivalent of the Queen's English. His mother, on the other hand, didn't appreciate it as much. While everyone who made it to Hong Kong was leaving behind the same oppressive forces, they each carried inside themselves a different shade of the same shadow.

During this time, Hing Him would take odd jobs on the weekend, sometimes washing dishes for a night in exchange for a special meal to feed his family, or working for the fishmonger for a large fish and maybe some crab and shrimp to take home as a treat. He would tell everyone he went fishing in the harbour, but his wife never believed him. Later in life, he told his youngest daughter, after she started writing freelance for local newspapers, that he used to sometimes write pieces for a small newspaper when he first arrived in Hong Kong. His wife would then chime in to confirm that he was never paid for those pieces. Eventually he took over his father's business as a manufacturer, subsequently trying—and failing—to pass on the family business to any of his children.

With the 1997 British handover of Hong Kong back to China looming, Cho Kei decided she was not going to wait around. She moved herself and her daughters to Canada in 1988, with the arrangement that her husband would stay behind and send money as needed. This arrangement was not uncommon for families like theirs, but being uncommon did not leave much room for solace. Cho Kei was left alone with her three daughters, ranging in age from six to seventeen, in a country she had only visited once on a whim. She didn't have an extended family of in-laws to contend with, but she also didn't speak either of this new country's official languages. At least here, however, her children had a better chance of thinking and feeling and speaking their minds. At least here, she could think and feel whatever she liked.

It took me twenty years to understand what my mother had done for me, for us. When I realized what she had sacrificed, I was scared to thank her, because I had never thought to do so until now. I didn't want it to be too late.

During those first few years of long summer nights in Edmonton, the family of four hung out in the coolness of their basement, where the television lived. Brown shag carpeting and plastic wood vinyl covered the floor and walls, accenting a massive woodland photo landscape. During that first year in Edmonton, I saw my mother cry for the first time in my life. Her eyes went bright red and her face scrunched up. We were watching television, and she was unable to hold it together any longer. Even though she was halfway around the world, her voice remained a whisper. We watched the television as it repeatedly showed a student standing in front of a moving tank in Beijing's

Tiananmen Square. My mother could no longer mask her emotions. It is the first time I see her scared. In her mother tongue, she asks no one in particular, *How can they keep doing this? How dare they open fire on all those students when the whole world is watching?* I don't know what to say or feel, because seeing your parent cry for the first time is more frightening than what they are crying about. I remember her reactions more than the event itself. I remember the fear that she feels in her body, so that I feel it in mine. My mother came to this country out of fear for herself and her children. The images flashing across the TV screen brought her fears back to the surface of her skin. The fact that she was thousands of kilometres away was only bittersweet consolation toward accepting her new life of isolation.

We visit Beijing together for the first time in 2012. A National Congress of the Communist Party of China is happening concurrently, and there are extra guards at every subway station and street corner. All of these junior cadets look unprepared to interrupt the unstoppable flow of human activity surrounding each checkpoint. We visit Tiananmen Square, where thousands of young people are posing with their peace signs and ear-to-ear smiles. We do not take any photos or smile. Cho Kei just wants her youngest daughter to see it, and then leave. She doesn't dare shake her head, but mutters under her breath, in English, that these people have no idea. *They are just standing here, and yet they have no idea what really happened here.* Cho Kei knows it's not just their youthful ignorance that allows them to smile like that. She has always described the government as lethal in every way. Her fears have become mine. My mother never used to talk about it, but after thirty years in Canada, she has begun. She has buried inside a deep mistrust. She never spoke about the past, because her body believes that someone might still be listening. People disappear. Historic events vanish. History books are wiped clean. This is what countries do, when the past is too shameful to face, the truth too frightening to bear. Our inability to speak about the past leads to a break—a rupture—in understanding everything that comes after.

It's 2017 and in an empty restaurant overlooking the Strait of Juan de Fuca, I order lunch for the both of us. Taking a day trip away from the hotel in James Bay, I had wanted to drive all the way to Port Renfrew and back, but my mother shook her head, saying it was too far, that we should head back. She's seventy-four and still travelling the world, but another hour to Port Renfrew is just too far in the wrong direction. Changing course from our plan of driving upward into the Interior, we settle on a short drive out for a meal at Sooke Harbour House.

Walking out onto the Strait, filling my lungs with whipped salty air, I momentarily give in to my drifting thoughts about living out here, about moving back west. Through the winding trees, I can see a white house standing alone across the harbour. The house calls to me, pulling me as close as I can stand at the edge of the rocky waters. The original plan was to drive up the island to see the show at the Nanaimo Art Gallery, but Cho Kei just wanted to spend some time with her daughter, who she sees only once or

33

twice a year. She asked me what kind of art would be there, and was disappointed when the response did not include landscape paintings by the Group of Seven. She liked Tom Thomson best, because in her adult art classes, he was framed as the wildest. I also wanted to visit Duncan, because of Indu, who told me about the city's history of a large Punjabi, Chinese, and Japanese population and their early relationship with the Cowichan against the British. She can only assume it was the Cowichan, as the Punjabi word for Indigenous people was *thaike*, which translates to *your father's older brother*, a patriarchal agrarian way of referring to the owners and custodians of the land. Depending on who is looking, be it a white male painter or a foreign-born logger, we will see the land differently. The physical history of this place, a knowledge that can stand and travel on its own, of the lives and accomplishments of racialized settlers and Indigenous nations, is almost non-existent in official capacities. Such a history travels only through word of mouth, through anecdotes, because unofficial histories can travel only through unofficial channels in unofficial languages.

At Harbour House, I order us a fresh garden salad with slabs of lightly seared tuna and peppery day-lily flowers. For my mother, a fisherman's boil overflowing with fresh mussels, their shiny dark shells smiling from her bowl. She shares bites of her catch of the day, and the golden layer of pan-seared skin across ribbons of silky, fatty salmon melts instantly in my mouth. As the seasonal sorbets of Alexander berry, pear, and quince scoops arrive, I ask her if she can sort out a few details for me. Our family lineage has never been clear, with each new fact uprooting an older one. As someone who has never seen myself reflected in the nation-state image of Canada, I have ceased looking, and instead started collecting my own stories.

I have always been under the impression that the maternal side of my family was rich, the paternal side poor. Neither of these impressions is true. After Mao, everyone who survived just was. I grew up thinking my maternal grandmother was the daughter of a diplomat, but a few years back it came out through an email from a cousin that there is a Wikipedia page about our great-grandfather. Sun Baoqi was the Republic of China's foreign minister, until he resigned over Japan's Twenty-One Demands in 1915. I look at his picture as a pixelated jpeg, his long beard, his nose. Do we look anything alike? His daughter is my grandmother, who married a prominent banker during the short-lived years of the Republic of China. I have seen photos of her on my mother's mahogany dresser, and I have realized, more than once, that I don't know how to recognize my own features.

Cho Kei is the youngest child of the first of her father's five wives. There would be twenty-four children in total, eight of whom were her full siblings. Her father died, Cho Kei recalls, when she was either two or three years old. As the Republic lost to the Communists, her mother and two of her siblings eventually moved from Beijing to Tianjin in 1954. By the height of Mao's Cultural Revolution, the Communist government and their legions of soldiers had taken everything from everyone by mobilizing those who had absolutely nothing. All bank accounts were frozen; untrained soldiers came stumbling into people's houses to take their clothes, rip up their floorboards, and physically damage and humiliate anyone with any previous shards of power or prestige. Families with wealth were forced to purchase government bonds, which would never become redeemable, in order to keep the economy afloat. Because of her family background, Cho Kei was not allowed to attend university and was sent to work at a school, where, for similar reasons, she was not allowed to teach history. It was at this school where she met Hing Him, whose family had been moving out of China and into Hong Kong as far back as 1949. With his previous girlfriend unwilling to leave China, and her first fiancé jailed in a work camp, they married each other and got ready to leave the mainland after their second daughter was born.

They stayed in Kowloon for sixteen years. Cho Kei never really grasped the Cantonese dialect. She understood the language, but could never speak it, and felt perpetually on the outskirts of the culture that surrounded her. I, on the other hand, grew up with the next generation's problems, hearing Mandarin from my parents and Cantonese from my siblings, school, and TV. I could understand both, but was incapable of separating their conflated intonations in my mind. Thus, I was unable to speak either. When my preschool started teaching us English vocabulary before I could walk, let alone talk, I stopped speaking altogether for a while. I couldn't translate what I heard to what I wanted to say, so I used as few words as possible.

In her family's first summer in Edmonton, Cho Kei enrolled all three of her daughters into English-language courses. She herself abstained. She felt too old and was still learning the last language, she would say self-deprecatingly. She would eventually have to learn English but was going to hold off for as long as she could. The great colonial project of the British Empire was just an addendum to how she was comprehending her world, whose farthest interiors and landscapes would never be touched by the rudimentary grasps of the English language's insufficient imagination to express beyond the primitive desire to possess all of its grammatical subjects.

Sprawl

"A First Nations woman who was hit by a trailer hitch, thrown from a passing car in Thunder Bay, Ont., last January, has died... The passenger in the car yelled, 'Oh, I got one,' after throwing the hitch at the sisters who were walking on McKenzie Street between Dease and Cameron streets."
—CBC News, 2017

"Reconciliation is not an Aboriginal problem; it is a Canadian one."
—from *Honouring the Truth, Reconciling for the Future: Summary of the Final Report of the Truth and Reconciliation Commission of Canada*, 2015

I buried my hamster north of 167A Avenue. I had never buried anything before. When my pet rabbits and turtles died in Kowloon, they simply disappeared. Out with the nightly trash. There being only levels of concrete terraces instead of fields. Freeways instead of fences. Fountains instead of ponds.

I walked along the big, empty street winding up to the convenience store, which stood at the edge of endless fields of weeds and trees and dirt piles. Kneeling down, I used my bare hands to dig a hole in the loose dirt small enough to fit the tiny cardboard coffin I had fashioned from an old decorative toy box. I never went back to visit the unmarked grave before roads were extended and subdivisions were built overtop of it.

In that last decade of the mighty twentieth century, Edmonton's most northern residential suburb was demarcated by a concrete slab of chiselled blue text welcoming you into the manufactured neighbourhood of Lake District. Turning east at the top of 97 Street before the road turned into Highway 28, Lake District was filled with cookie-cutter four-level splits and working-class families. The land, having been developed exponentially, no longer had the same sense of isolation that, for better or for worse, went hand in hand with a sense of exploration.

We walked. In large circles. June, her older sister, May, and me. We walked around all night. We would walk until it was pure silence and not a single car could be heard or pair of headlights seen. We became fast friends as neighbourhood kids in the same sleepy cul-de-sac. June and I were in the same grade, but I got along better with May, who was already in junior high. Their mom had passed away, and their dad, heartbroken, decided to move the kids to Edmonton for a fresh start.

I never knew that our elementary school's name, Lago Lindo, actually referred to something beyond the soccer league of the same name. Spanish for Pretty Lakes. Development around synthetic lakes. It was a neighbourhood where I learned to make fast friends with girls and boys who liked to play with no adult supervision in sight. I learned to forget what I knew about quick cars and suspicious adults who try to go through your pockets or lead you away in bustling crowds.

There were no crowds here. Just wide-open space.

We had regular sleepovers at May and June's house since their dad often worked the night shift. We ate crackers with microwaveable cheese and invited anyone who was willing for all-nighters of video games and, eventually, other things. We got our preteen hands on sugary booze and smokes and VHS tapes of huge cocks and shaved cunts, and we wanted to share our bounty with strange boys and stranger girls. Once midnight passed and the neighbourhood slept, the three of us went for long walks, restless, with no destination. Past silent trails and quiet houses. We strolled through empty fields where we would stop and lie down to stare undisturbed into the dark blue dome of speckled stars. We walked to the edge of Lago Lindo, past empty roads behind trees and fields with straw bales where horses still ran wild. We walked through Kilkarney and meandered our way to Londonderry. On one of these aimless summer nights, we met a short boy named Len and followed him to a deserted mall parking lot. His friends were already there skating up and down the mezzanine ramps and they had something to show us. Len's taller friend smiled and stuck out his swollen tongue where a metal ball perched on top like a silver pearl. None of us had seen anything like that before. We watched as he unscrewed the ball from its shaft with his stained fingertips. He sucked the shaft clean of puss and put the ball back in. His skinny arms stuck out in sharp angles from a ratty band T-shirt, and his charcoal-lined eyes looked out from behind clumps of dark, matted hair. He used his spit to clean the piercing, and I remembered the warning, the feeling in the pit of my stomach that emanated from my mother warning me about teenage boys—*a couple of Indians*, she had whispered, recalling with shame and disgust how they had spat on her from a mall escalator. My mother believed that, being Chinese, she was an easier target than the white people around her. There is a hierarchy to racism, my mother had warned, and in this country, whiteness firmly sat at the top. I didn't know what to think of these boys, who were mostly too shy to make eye contact. June would go on to date Len for a summer, before he disappeared, with rumours he got sent to juvie. Maybe he was just sent to live with his dad. Either way, she moved on pretty quickly. The streets belonged to no one in subdivisions that hosted everyone. More often than not, we started to share the road with semi trucks cutting through town, flashing their headlights and pulling their horns, the only lights and sounds on these late-night walks. We saw nobody else on the wide-open streets, and when we did, we ran.

If you looked at a map of Edmonton in the mid 1990s, locating the long, straight road of 170 Street, and traced a finger to the very southern tip where the road suddenly stopped at 62 Avenue, that was Wanyandi Road. Moving for the fifth time in six years, I was now living minutes away from what was then the "largest mall in the world." West Edmonton Mall would eventually lose its title and become just the largest mall in Canada, reduced to another Alberta roadside attraction vying for attention alongside a half-ton pysanka and other gigantic sculptures of a beaver, pierogi, kubasa, and dozens more larger-than-life structures dotting small towns and secondary highways.

With this move to a visibly wealthy suburb, all of my new classmates and friends came from new money and did not like going for long walks, because they never had to. The sidewalks were all new, brick-lined with red-and-brown cement and paired with the standardized grey-blue cedar fencing of the nearby country club, where class could be bought where it was not bred. It was common for sidewalks to wrap around elongated blocks as decorative markers more than functional paths, only to suddenly come to an abrupt end with no rhyme or reason. Dog walkers were the only consistent pedestrians with morning and evening routines, and I found myself following them to know the trails. In the guileless summer days, when I had no structure and no real friends, I went out for walks in the middle of the day and lay in the field behind my house, looking up at the sky, surveying my new surroundings, and seeing nothing but cookie-cut-out shadows all around me. I had never felt more alone.

In the evenings, I looked out from my bedroom window and watched as cars pulled into their respective garages, which opened and shut in a snap. After all the double- and triple-car garages had been filled back up and the barely distinguishable scents of dinner had passed, the flicker of television sets began radiating out from the windows of every house. For a few years, there was an annual end-of-summer block party, where my neighbours convened annually to share store-bought potato salad from the same grocery store. It would be the only time I ever saw people standing on our street.

To this day, the transit lines have never expanded and new sidewalks were never added. As soon as someone turned sixteen and could drive, bus rides were no longer necessary or desired. It was the kind of neighbourhood where affluence was new and prominently displayed through the latest models of luxury sedans and SUVs. I never made any new friends in that neighbourhood that stuck past a year, and carpooling to school was never even an option. Shortly after I moved out, my mother sold the big empty house she had designed for cheap. She caught the market during the peak of a boom cycle and retired to Vancouver. She was always smart with money that way: trading up properties, reducing her small business's overhead before selling it for a profit, and never holding any consumer debt. She asked me to come with her to Vancouver, but for the first time in my life, I had the choice to stay. So I stayed.

To fulfill one of the last university courses required for graduation, I signed up for a community placement that took me up and down 95 Street, 142 Street, Stony Plain Road, and anywhere else the organization had registered street-based sex workers in their database. I signed up because I wanted to know my new neighbours. I had moved to the area of 118 Avenue and regularly saw women working all around me. I knew a lot of people, mostly artists and young families, moving into the area, and we all suspected several of the houses nearby were drug dens or flophouses. A couple of times I woke up to pleading and banging on my front door from some spillover from the house across the street, asking if I knew when they would be home and if I had anything they could have. I learned to stop answering the door, as I never had what they were looking for.

My placement involved a ride-along in a dark blue van cruising down the Avenue of Champs. Avenue of Nations. Until we ran out of supplies. Pulling over here. Turning around there. Checking in with young women who spat out their names and dates of birth so fast I always had to ask them to repeat more slowly. Most of the sex workers know what they want: Lube. Flavoured condoms. Something to drink. Something to eat. For the van to move on, as its presence scares away the johns. Most of them are really young. Too young to tell you their real age, but old enough to memorize new dates of birth when asked. The

45

faces I see are all cis and trans Indigenous women. Lorna, who supervises the ride-along, tells me what two-spirit means to her people. I tell her that makes sense to me.

Before getting my licence and a car I could call my own, I drove around with Tyler and his buddies. He had frosted tips and a big, sad smile. He and Billy and George were friends, and they loved going for pleasure cruises in George's tank of an all-American black bruiser cruiser. George was a tall, lanky kid from British immigrants who loved Wu-Tang Clan, and he named his car a racist slur that we all shook our heads at but never pushed him about. One night, gunning his engine at a light, he shouted at a car full of young black men about how his Ol' N———was faster than theirs. He got his dumb white ass chased around that night, and unfortunately, but deservedly for us, Tyler, Billy, and I were also in the car. Billy couldn't stop laughing as he was finally living out his *Dukes of Hazzard* fantasies. I was sitting in the back with Tyler and could see he had turned paler than usual. Though I was the only girl, he was still the smallest and weakest person in the car, and he knew it. George eventually lost his tail in the deep and winding suburbs of west Edmonton after a prolonged and reckless pursuit. As high school graduation neared, I started to drift off from them. Tyler still liked hanging out with George and Billy, as he really enjoyed driving up and down 97 Street with them, flicking pennies at sex workers. He invited me along a few times, all the while snapping his fingers to mime flicking a penny out of a moving vehicle.

After I got my licence, I spent years letting Simon drive us around. I would drive to his house and he would drive us around for the rest of the night. Simon's dad identified as Native—not Indigenous, not Aboriginal, but Native. Of which nation it was never clear. I just remember how their family room displayed a buffalo head larger than the one at the museum. What was clear was how he had put himself through law school. On the application, where it asked you to check if you were Aboriginal, he didn't. *No handouts. I'm no fucking Indian*, he proudly told his son. One summer night with nothing else to do, Simon drove us around town in his dad's SUV, listening to Depeche Mode's *Ultra* and smoking with the windows down. Sirens were blaring and I had long forgotten this part of the city. *I love this part of the city*, he said. People shouting and running down the middle of streets. Simon never knew I grew up just north of here. To him, we were a couple of bored suburbanites looking for a bit of the real city. We saw a lot of women working that night. Simon, in hushed tones between drags, felt the need to confess how he had been disappearing at night. Almost every night. Finally he admitted how he had been coming down here. *Nothing ever happened, though*, Simon said, looking over, trying to reassure me of some moral ground I didn't know we had shared. He *just wanted to see these women*, he said, but he *would never do anything with them.*

There are no women in sight until 114 Avenue. Wiry silhouettes in clothes that don't fit onto their bodies. Standing. Often leaning. With one hand on their hip and the other hitching a ride. Waving down cars and family minivans with baby seats in the back and crosses hanging from the rear-view mirrors. Every morning as I waited for the bus, I watched johns pick up women against faded storefronts during rush hour. They'll turn away once they see you're not a potential date. Though some will still wave at you. Stare back at you.

Before moving to the neighbourhood of 118 Avenue, I walked around a lot with Monty. He renamed himself Monty when he moved to the city from Red Deer. New city, new identity. He wore striped sweaters and a baseball cap to hide his bald patch, which he hid only from himself and not the young girls in his poetry classes. He liked Edmonton. This part of Edmonton. The old Edmonton with a small-town feel. Less concrete. More storefronts. Mom-and-pop businesses with dilapidated signs next to painted polar bears and football murals. Boarded-up places next to Grand Opening signs next to moneylenders next to Portuguese bakeries.

I continued to walk through the neighbourhood after moving in, despite countless run-ins with johns. On the first really nice weekend of the post-snow spring, I was propositioned by four different men within a two-block radius—johns in vehicles driving a little too close, yelling out of their windows, expecting me to be working. Wounded when I told them to fuck off, their response was always surprise first, anger second, flabbergasted and huffing, *Then why are you even walking around here?* as they peeled off.

A new neighbourhood arts café banned sex workers from

coming into their business shortly after they opened their doors. The café was the first of many new businesses to reopen along the newly revitalized "Arts Avenue" of 118 and one of the few businesses open after 6:00 p.m. that wasn't a pawnshop or moneylender. The café was connected to a new arts festival trying to "clean up" the area's image with open mics and painting exhibitions. Cycling through an endless supply of Christian folk rock and acrylic self-portraits and watercolour lilies, it would appear as if the neighbourhood's existing social dynamics were being forced out through the sheer power of mediocrity. The café didn't last, but the street-level drug use and sex work only became more concentrated through these civic revitalization efforts.

I dropped Lorna off after each of our shared shifts. Coming to a stop at 114 Avenue, Lorna smiled and waved bye for now from the sidewalk. *Stay safe,* I blurted out. We had spent the afternoon editing, printing, and stapling warnings about another bad date—a real estate agent who had allegedly been picking up sex workers in the area, driving them way out of the city limits, and violently assaulting them. Lorna knew the cops always took precautions not to leak a good lead, using the women on the streets as bait until they could build up enough of a case. Catching one violent assaulter does nothing to stop the cycle. And to catch one means to lose more than one.

When I first landed in Edmonton, my family spent a short summer in a downtown apartment. In the evenings we walked along Jasper Avenue and toward the river valley.

On our walks back in Kowloon, I was given coins to hand to the men and women silently begging on street corners. *They're less fortunate than us,* I had been told. I was never given any coins after moving to Canada. My mother's new acquaintances, other first generation immigrants she would meet, all said the same thing: *It's not our place to help them. The government keeps them that way so that they can't take back their land.*

I saw the same woman walking up and down 95 Street long before I knew her name. Short hair framing a hard face. Quick eyes. A mouth as sharp as a blade liquefying into babble. She walked with a hobble, which she waved away as damage by past lovers, parents, and foster parents. When I last saw her, Meg had just come from a fight with her roommate, who had called her a string of bad names, like slut and whore. Meg even suspected her roommate might be trying to poison her daughter, who had epileptic seizures now and then—like when the roommate had a date directly across the room. Meg was really upset that day. She just needed a place to stay for a while—explaining her band had a cheque for her that would be delivered the following week. She could pick up a date if we couldn't find her a bed. She exuded endless warmth and could crack anyone up. When she heard about the latest violent offender on the loose, she chuckled at his physical description, thinking how funny he must look. She was quick to add that those women who got themselves killed probably deserved it, because that's what happens when you rip those guys off.

Theresa was new to the city when she started working at the drop-in centre. Moving there from the east coast, she kept her radio tuned to Aboriginal Voices Radio Network. Theresa reminded me of June, whom I probably wouldn't recognize anymore. Sometimes Lorna and Theresa would sit in the office at the end of the day and talk with each other. Never over each other. They talked about tradition. What they knew and what they were learning. What the next generation was retaining. How knowledge keeps getting passed regardless of the systems in place. They talked about angel readings. Spirits. Natural medicines. Theresa got excited by something she heard that morning on the radio, about a healer researching the biochemical connections between physics and the spirit. They agreed that one should never talk about spiritual matters at night. I listened to them, quietly, in the corner while I sorted the donated dry groceries onto makeshift shelves. The office got a steady stream of regulars, sometimes new faces, but often they were familiar to Lorna. Almost always after Lorna introduced me as a new volunteer, a woman I had never seen before would say, *Yeah, we've already met.* I never asked when and where, but nodded, *Yes, it is nice to see you again.*

Venture

We drove down and up the flatness of Highway 2 together. It was just for one year, between 2006 and 2007, when I worked for her at Venture Publishing. I was twenty-five years old. I had been hired as the events and marketing assistant, and it would be the first and last corporate job I ever held. Power breakfasts, golf tournaments, networking symposiums—I organized dozens of these events for the *nouveau riche* of Alberta's oil and gas industries, and was surprisingly good at it.

Until I wasn't.

On my last day of work, Ruth and I made a friendly hundred-dollar bet as to whether I would work a nine-to-five job ever again. That was the last time we spoke to each other.

In that one year, I drove thousands of klicks and learned how to take shortcuts on a straight road. But a few thousand kilometres each year was nothing for Ruth. At her busiest, she was travelling between Edmonton and Calgary at least once a week. She always had a suitcase packed and ready—she was practical that way. Ruth was known in business-elite circles for her outrageous fashion sense, but I remembered her as someone who rarely wore shoes. Padding around the office in stockings, she would blow down the hallways and stairwells of Venture like a gale-force wind; there was nothing more intimidating than the stealth attack of Ruth's stockinged feet suddenly appearing at the edge of your desk.

I didn't know who Ruth was until I applied to work for her. I knew hers was a name that other people recognized. I had never read any of her company's trade magazines or heard her rousing speeches to blinking and bearded journalism students. I had been freelance writing for just over five years and was in the midst of narrowing my field, from culture to contemporary art. These nuances did not exist in Edmonton, but I had not yet learned this information. After completing an undergraduate degree in literature and film at the University of Alberta, I worked odd jobs, from kitchen duties at the Blue Plate Diner to being an office manager for a non-profit memorial-planning service. Neither job alone paid the bills, but I got to eat for free on the weekends and learned that almost everyone, no matter their age or background, was unprepared for death.

Like many of my peers who were consciously choosing to stay, I, too, had bought a house in central Edmonton. I bought a tiny one-bedroom bungalow for $170,000 and sold it for not much more seven years later. No one ever talked about race or class in Edmonton. Whether one's family had money or not, was born in Edmonton or not, the shared dream was to lease a new car, own your own home, and run your own small business.

I learned from the pages of Ruth's business magazines that the corridor between Edmonton and Calgary held North America's highest concentration of small businesses, and their owners lived and breathed and worked their way to self-made economic prosperity. No one I knew ever talked about class divisions; they just named different neighbourhoods. A multitude of worlds lived between the suburban divisions of Old Glenora, Belvedere, or Mill Woods. The city as a whole, with its denim-clad and Sorel-footed swagger, had a sure sense of itself as a place for the entrepreneurial working-class. I was in my mid-twenties, but even then I knew I didn't want to work for anyone else—especially not in the arts. A typical turn through an arts festival had left me feeling exploited and burnt-out, a feeling since perpetuated under different charity numbers in different cities over the years. I knew I wanted something else, but, already weighed down by a mortgage and car bills in a resource-extraction economy, I couldn't see a way out.

In the days leading up to my new job, I had only known one person to offer their opinions on Ruth. He was a former journalism student who saw the end of the industry coming and began training to be a Red Seal carpenter. He warned me about Ruth, using words like *ruthless* and *domineering*. I would hear these descriptions many times over the years about women in leadership positions, but

I hadn't noticed at the time that such words always came from men, young and old. I was, however, already aware of my brief history working exclusively for these kinds of women, and wondered if such names were all there was to aspire to.

Ruth commanded the rooms in which she stood, and whether she was right or wrong, rude or not, people listened. I didn't idolize her, not by any stretch, but I listened, too. Ruth was the first person to ask me just *whom* was I trying to reach through my writing. If I was going to stubbornly insist on writing only about the arts, what kind of platforms and audiences was I aiming for? Did I think about whether there would ever be an audience large enough for my ambitions? In those three hour car rides up and down the corridor, Ruth also taught me to never send a cold pitch to an editor, to always introduce myself first, and to ease into a story pitch only if and when a response came back. This advice would eventually lead me away from Ruth, away from the stability I had felt for a year, and send me hurtling toward the life I have now. In many ways, Ruth saved me from what I thought I needed to be.

For each event I coordinated for Venture, averaging one or two per month, I created corresponding binders that lined my office shelf previously filled by event coordinators before me. I updated all of the marketing details—mostly just the date and year—booked conference rooms, arranged hotel rooms for attending staff members, and prepared outlines of the menu for Ruth to approve. Sales took care of all sponsorship arrangements, and I was left in charge of setup and teardown, and all the logistics in between. Midway through completing exactly one year's worth of events, I was already wondering how many more years of this I could possibly do before growing numb. The biggest event I was tasked with organizing was Venture's tenth-anniversary party, which, being a unique event, also came with no binders and no predetermined guidelines, and thus, was my favourite kind of event to organize. I rented the old Aviation Museum—an empty airplane hangar—booked a couple of local bands and DJs, set up some memory lane through ten years of publishing, hired my friends as caterers and bartenders, and made sure that, above all, Ruth was happy. By evening's end, having been feted all night by some of the province's most accomplished women and men, Ruth danced in her stocking feet on the portable dance floor, Scotch in hand. She looked happy.

Venture launched yet another new print magazine, one aimed at millennials in Alberta's corporate workforce. Market research indicated that most millennials would change careers at least five times in their life, and prioritize their work-life balance over climbing the corporate ladder. Millennials would be the most educated generation yet, and possibly the least interested in following in their parents' footsteps. I wrote some of the magazine's snappy copy, but could never convince myself that this was what I wanted to be doing. The millennial magazine only persisted for a blip, having never made the successful transition into an online entity.

Over the course of my time at Venture, where I made more

money than I had ever made in my life, aggressively paying off my mortgage and renting out my basement suite, I began moonlighting as a freelance arts writer. I felt able to take a risk. I felt I had to take a risk. Fed up with my editors at the local weeklies who twisted my words back into press releases, I stopped writing for print publications and started publishing my own writing online. By 2007, blogs had exploded into mainstream media, crossing over into the realm of pop-cultural references. *Prairie Artsters* started as a way to share canned articles and grew quickly into reviews and interviews every week. When I first met my then-editor Steven in his airless office at *See Magazine*, I remember him telling me through his collapsed nasal cavity that nobody wanted to read about the visual arts in this city, let alone read critical reviews. Steven was echoing what my very first editor, Chad, from the Edmonton *Journal*, had also said: nobody wanted to read criticism about themselves or their friends.

That fall, everything changed. I drove Joyce, Venture's then-associate publisher, to one of our symposiums in Canmore. As a not-so-recent transplant from Toronto, Joyce had never seen the Rocky Mountains. Prior to moving to Alberta, she had also been a vegetarian. Driving past Calgary during the city's sprawling rush hour, she pointed in the general vicinity of the Rockies and said, *I see them.* She had no idea. As we pressed on through Bow Valley Trail and night fell over us, the houses dropped off, one by one. The river disappeared and the trees thickened. We were surrounded by looming, jagged shadows pressing down around us. Joyce's phone service became sparse. Our co-workers ahead of us had taken a wrong turn somewhere between Bragg Creek and Kananaskis. We were alone on the highway with only intermittent radio cutting in and out of our silence. Joyce grew increasingly anxious, as she had never before felt so isolated through landscape. Feeling her fear, I understood something new about geography and our psyches as I calmly steered us toward our remote destination.

A day into the mountains, I received a message from David, my new editor at *Vue Weekly*. *Vue* was an independent newsprint publication with a small but steadfast circulation and a masthead of young editors who cared about the city and each other enough to generously offer critical feedback about local politics, businesses, and the arts. A few months after I'd launched *Prairie Artsters*, David approached me about wanting to turn it into an arts column for him. These were the last days when people still picked up print over online publications, when a blog could be turned into print to *increase* readership. He was baby-faced, fresh from editing the University of Alberta's student newspaper, and, as with most young editors, he was overly professional and precocious in tone. But his email that morning was rambling, not at all like usual. He was emotional but trying not to be. He was writing to let his freelancers know that Ross, the news editor at *Vue*, who was our colleague and friend, had suddenly passed away. A memorial service was to be held in a few days, and everyone was welcome to pay their respects.

In a separate message, I pressed David for what little

information he had. All he knew was that Ross had jumped off the High Level Bridge. He was twenty-four years old.

Within a month of Ross's memorial, I handed in my resignation at Venture. Something inside me had snapped. It was like being jolted awake from a deep slumber. I had finally found a small community of writers and editors who I believed in, and who believed in me, but as I then projected in my narcissistic grief, maybe they didn't believe in themselves. My life progressed before me with a house, a car, a job with a corporate credit card, but I never felt fulfilled. I woke up and realized I didn't want any of it. Ruth tried to convince me otherwise, to hold off my resignation until the shock had passed. What she never understood was that I was mourning my life as it was. Death is a recalibration for the living.

By the end of the year, I had left my short-lived corporate career and gone into freelancing full-time. I left Venture because I was unhappy with my life. Looking back, I was depressed for most of my adult life while living in Edmonton. No matter what I did, I never felt like I fit in. On subsequent return trips, I still feel invisible in a city that has also moved on. I have associated my past depression with an entire city, which I know is unfair to a place that keeps changing, but when Gilbert, another local freelance arts writer, jumped off the High Level Bridge, I knew it was my time to leave Edmonton entirely.

I have lived with depression to varying degrees, but unless someone directly confides in me, I have never been able to identify that someone else was going through their own depression. There are signs, but they vary from person to person, depending on their specific circumstances. I never saw it coming with Ross, or Gilbert, and certainly not with Ruth.

When I heard about Ruth, it had been ten years since I had left my job at Venture. My mind refused to believe it. It felt impossible. In the weeks that followed, I read every article and obituary I could find. A lot of people were angry at the *Edmonton Journal* for saying it was death by suicide. She was sixty years old.

Ted was the first person to break the news to me. He has known me since before I worked for Venture, and who knew Ruth, because everyone did. He remembered seeing me on my last day of work there, walking by the restaurant he was sitting in with the biggest smile on my face.

I remember that day, too. I felt free. For that moment, I felt happy.

The Bridge

"This is the High Level Bridge. This is where people from Edmonton go when we're finally ready to kill ourselves."

These are the opening words in Trevor Anderson's 2010 short film, *The High Level Bridge*. The film did quite well as an independent release, screening at the Toronto International Film Festival, Sundance, and AFI in Los Angeles, and was even shown as an installation in the Alberta Biennial. Trevor's voice, in his usual on-camera *I-know-something-you-don't* intonation, recalls anonymous friends who have jumped or encountered jumpers. To this day, I find their anonymity difficult to endure.

In the three years it took to construct the High Level Bridge in Edmonton, Alberta, the winter seasons proved to be the most efficient for the construction workers; there is no time to waste in a prairie winter. The High Level Bridge was one of the first bridges in western Canada that served not just the rail, but also streetcar service, passenger vehicles, and pedestrians. It was not the only bridge of its kind, or unique in any other way, but it was Edmonton's first iconic structure, and it hangs large in the city's psyche.

Olive Marie Poncella Beauchamp was born on April 21, 1935, on the High Level Bridge. As a general interest story, the *Journal* ran a contest to name the baby, with a ten-dollar trust. Over one thousand submissions came in, with Poncella, roughly meaning *this one from the bridge*, being selected by the child's parents—presumably for the cash, or maybe just to fit into a new city, which was most new to itself.

Olive, or "Cella," "Punch," "Punchie" to her friends, like most everyone else, eventually left Edmonton. In 1967, she moved east with her then-husband, Earl, and their two daughters. That same year, Annette Beres (formerly La Riviere), now of Richmond, BC, who at twelve years old had submitted the winning name of Poncella, tried to publicly search for the whereabouts of the bridge baby.

I came across this information when I was searching the city archives for any human-interest files related to the High Level Bridge. The archivist made a sad face when I mentioned that I was aware of how many suicides occurred on the bridge. Her face lit up, though, when she found the file on Olive Beauchamp.

Though Punchie passed away in Halifax in 2015, her

obituary ran in the *Edmonton Journal,* fondly recalling the legacy of being the first bridge baby. From her obit, I learned that Punchie's father left his wife to raise their two kids by herself in Edmonton. She worked at the Great Western Garment Company, sewing zippers into jeans. Likely many a pair of Red Strap denims—a popular brand of jeans—had passed through her fingers. These jeans would eventually become the namesake of a short-lived art market and four-storey empty warehouse space that hosted the local printmaking community, as well as one-off events and art shows by the likes of dancer and choreographer Kathy Ochoa. The space never really functioned as a hospitable studio, and was rumoured to serve more as glorified storage for its owner and local architect, Gene Dub, who had a soft spot for saving scraps of forgotten civic history.

As a teenager, my then-best friend and I would go do gut checks on the High Level Bridge. How did it feel to stand on the bridge? Was life still worth living as the river rushed below? While I refused to go on antidepressants, I was always distracting myself with other substances. Life was fine as long as I was not sober.

In spring 2009, I joined in the search for the body of a colleague who was last spotted heading toward the High Level Bridge. It had been days since anyone had heard from him. Organizers told everyone to meet at the Butter-dome and to get themselves into teams of three. I teamed up with Gerry and Holly, and only one of us truly believed we would find Gilbert alive. One out of three Edmontonians had hope. We combed the area just above Kinsmen, from the road down to the river. We came across piles of garbage and several clearings with clothes and sleeping bags bunched up into the bushes. Gilbert was the first arts writer I had ever read. In Edmonton. In the world. I never knew how we were all just trying to manage our depression the best ways we could. I only saw him as another freelance writer, attending every opening, like I did. I started writing about art because I thought I could do it better. He was gregarious with those he knew and quiet around those he knew less. I later found out that, shortly before disappearing, Gilbert had been let go from one of his regular writing gigs. I wondered and worried if I was going to turn out just like him—except when I attended his memorial, I realized I didn't really know anything about him.

Three deaths were reported during the bridge's construction, but only two names ever surfaced. Christian Olson, who had arrived from Norway a few months earlier, died by accident in 1909. His name was mentioned in his widow, Barbara's, 1953 obituary. Luke McDonough, from the nearby town of Lacombe, died in 1910 from an encounter with a piledriver. He had been working for only six days before his accident. He was twenty-six years old. The third name has not been found in any archive. I asked Trevor if he knew the name, but he doesn't recall. We have both heard rumours about a body preserved in one of the bridge's cement pillars, but nothing official ever turned up.

In 1934, an astrologer predicted the bridge would collapse on November 1 of that year. People gathered at either end to watch the catastrophe, but none came in the form they were expecting.

Peter Jacobs, twelve, fell to his death in 1954. The structure of the bridge was inviting for urban climbers and pigeon hunters. The provincial coroner had to issue a public statement warning parents to not let their children climb the bridge, especially along the girders and latticework.

In 2010, I was walking south on the bridge and saw a figure out of the corner of my eye, just under the southwest side of the trusses below the University of Alberta. He appeared to be a middle-aged, chubby, balding white man with oily glasses. His tongue was sticking out as he stood there huffing and jerking off, looking up at me. His pants were off, but because of the climate he was still wearing a thick, scratchy-looking sweater. I yelled, *I see you!* which only made his motions more vigorous.

When I briefly lived on 110 Street, my balcony faced the northwest side of the legislature and the mouth of the High Level Bridge. At least once a week, I would watch large sixteen- and twenty-wheeled trucks stall the impatient traffic behind them by having to reverse up the hill when they realized they couldn't make the bridge's low 3.2-metre clearance.

I didn't have a cellphone for most of my life in Edmonton. Neither did Paul, or Claire, or anyone back then who had seen someone jump. In his film, Trevor recounts his friend finding a random cellphone on the bridge, most likely from somebody biting it on the ice and losing their phone as they fell. Trevor's friend picked up the phone right before coming upon a stranger ready to jump. He used the found phone to call 911 and talked to the stranger until help arrived. The next day, the owner of the phone was told about the heroics of losing their phone in the right place at the right time. More often than not, though, this is not the way things turn out.

Trevor dedicated his film to "R.M." and I asked him years later why he didn't name Ross. He politely answered, but I can't seem to recall the reasoning, because there is no logic in who lives and who dies and whose stories we are really telling. Ross had allegedly checked himself into the University of Alberta Hospital. After being released, he headed for the bridge. I last saw him at an art opening at Latitude 53. He was leaving the gallery as I was entering. We made a dumb joke about something. I remember laughing.

Over the decades, the streetcar on the top deck was removed piece by piece, first having its trolley wires cut in 1958, before finally ceasing operation altogether in 1967. The railway followed and has been out of commission since 1989. Vehicle traffic on the lower deck has been one-way southbound since its six-month closure in 1995. The seasonal sixty-metre waterfall ended in 2014. And in 2016, new suicide-prevention barriers were installed across the two-kilometre-long crossing, cagelike and bent inward. Suicides on the bridge have gone down, but numbers remain high across the province as prevention and admittance remain taboo topics.

A second bridge baby would be born on October 30, 1938, with far less public interest. Rushing to the Misericordia Community Hospital from New Sarepta, a hamlet inside of present-day Leduc largely settled by Moravian Brethren Germans from the Russian diaspora, the Priers' family car met a haze of smoke, and the second—and last—recorded bridge baby would be born. The *Journal* ran another contest, with another ten-dollar trust, and out of five hundred submissions, Mrs. I. E. McFarlane's "Levhila" would become Levila Elizabeth Prier. Purportedly meaning *high level* in Latin, *Lav hila*, I am also told, translates from Hindi to English as *love moments*. In Bosnian, *lev* means *lion*; in Hebrew, *heart*. In a postwar profile that focused on how beautiful Levila had become, the journalist noted that she became a stenographer for the Department of Highways in Edmonton, and that she would be cashing out that trust soon, as she could really use the money.

The High Level Bridge has been a one-way road for decades.

No matter where I go or where I have been, driving across the High Level Bridge remains one of the most perfect experiences. The bridge is guarded by black metal trusses, and the light and wind still breaks through from the North Saskatchewan below. A valley of green stretches out, or, if you're lucky enough to be around for that one week when summer plummets into winter, a plethora of red and gold—the scent of death and foliage is pungent. In winter, the matte black of the bridge resists the snowdrifts that collect against its rivets. In these colder months, the High Level Bridge, like the rest of the city's sentiments, shrinks away from the sub-zero temperatures, shortening the structure by up to two feet. Driving across again, the car wheels hit that familiar rattle. A low, echoing hum reverberates inside the car, inside my mind, my chest. Crossing the bridge takes less than a minute, but in that moment I remember everything.

Treaties 2, 4, 5, 6, 8, 10

I woke up at the crack of dawn, even though the farm had long since had a rooster to crow. The bristling silence of wind had shaken me from sleep, waking everything inside the lonesome farmhouse without even a tree to shield it. I had never been to Saskatchewan before. On a whim, I had accepted Donna's invitation to drive out to her family farm for a long weekend over the summer. The drive from Edmonton took the better part of a day, not counting stops made along the way in North Battleford and Swift Current, plus a detour to Moose Jaw to see where Donna grew up.

The farm had bore her family's name for as long as Donna could remember. Titled after her Scottish predecessors, who came over in the late 1800s, the farm, like so much land across the Prairies, had been measured out and given away to legions of white, able-bodied men from all over Europe who were willing to settle this place in the name of Canada.

The farm was tucked between a maze of secondary highways, near the tiny town of Tugaske, which flexed five streets wide by three streets deep, butting up against the 367 but staying off the main road of 42. Sitting right between the towns of Eyebrow and Elbow, the farm stretched for fewer hectares than it used to when the fields were still tended, but it remained a sizable plot of land.

All this land.

Donna's grandma Agnes spent her entire life on this land. Born close to the beginning of the twentieth century, she lived on the farm until almost the dawn of the twenty-first. After her kids grew up and her husband passed, she stayed on the farm all the same. With just Agnes living there, the mice moved in to keep her company, taking over the entire upstairs with periodic visits to the kitchen. She refused to move closer to any city or change anything about how she lived. Near the end of her life, her fifty-plus-year-old son and daughter-in-law moved onto the land, squatting in a trailer until it was their time to take over the family farm. Agnes lived her whole life believing that the land beneath her feet was her birthright, as did many of her generation. At the last big family reunion, with all her children and grandchildren around her, Agnes gave everyone a plastic vial filled with dirt from the farm, so they could all take a bit of home with them wherever they went.

As much as she loved her grandma, Donna threw out that vial a long time ago.

With a sparse population of one million spread out over 650,000 square kilometres, Saskatchewan is roughly the same size in land mass as Afghanistan, with a difference in population density of roughly 34 million people. Saskatchewan is pictorially known for its vast wheat fields of gold in the summer and endless sheets of white in the winter. In the 1950s and 1960s, having nowhere else to go, the American art critic Clement Greenberg began a series of visits to northern Saskatchewan, attracting a higher than normal concentration of postwar Modernist painters and sculptors to Emma Lake's summer workshops, as they "discovered" the ideal realization of flatness in form and embodiment in the surrounding landscape. The legacies of this abstractionist influence echoed down for decades, reverberating from Edmonton to Winnipeg, shaping university fine arts curricula as well as the visual identities of these cities through brutalist architecture and public art while reinforcing the false superiority of a European aesthetic.

As we drove down and across grids of highways, the hills straightened out and the trees disappeared. Just when I thought the roads were as flat as they could get, they managed to get even flatter. I had never seen this kind of open space before, buoyed by horizon on all sides. Donna laughed at my sense of awe and remembered when her family briefly hosted a foreign exchange student from South Korea. He had ridden silently in the car from the airport, continually snapping photos of the nothingness all around him. I fought the same urge to take bad photographs of the vastness that surrounded us. I knew photographs needed scale and perspective to make sense, but those elements were deeply entombed inside of me. I have never been so physically reminded of the cramped quarters of Kowloon than when under the open skies of Saskatchewan. Not in the glass skyline of downtown Vancouver or the packed subway cars during Toronto's rush hour. But here: sitting on a rock in an empty farm field in the middle of Saskatchewan. Here I was aware of the sensation of having zero personal space in which to breathe. Being in its diametrical opposite, I could learn to feel the other.

Bad photographs of open skies and a couple of straw bales would eventually appear in a national magazine standing in for all of Saskatchewan. A Toronto-based editor asked me if I could write a feature on a province-wide art project in its earliest stages, and if I could also supply some photographs. It did not seem to matter to anyone that I did not live there or know anything of its history. It would be my first shot at writing a national feature, so I took it. The article focused on a group of curators and artists from Saskatoon, Regina, and Prince Albert who wanted to shape their province into the next Münster, a major international art event that happened every ten years in and around a small town in Germany. There was a lot of space and numerous abandoned towns throughout Saskatchewan, which the curators thought would be exciting to offer up to international artists from countries like India and Brazil, who were presumed to have never had access to such unlimited scales of land.

Saskatchewan's land mass is covered by six separate treaties, predominantly Treaty 10 in the north, Treaty 6 in the centre, and Treaty 4 in the south. Treaty 4, otherwise known as the Qu'Appelle Treaty of 1874, came into being much later than the securing of Treaty 1 at Fort Garry, in what is now known as Winnipeg. Coupled with the beginning of the railroad expansion from west to east that would shape everything in between, the Crown took land as needed, when it suited their opportunities for expansion— which continues to be Canada's approach to treating Indigenous nations and their needs as afterthoughts. When the Crown needed land, they took it through treaty-making, which under international law is understood as a nation-to-nation agreement. But consistently, the Crown has threatened Indigenous nations and their people into wards of the state, challenging their assertion for self-determination and Aboriginal title, repeatedly attempting to destroy their languages and knowledge, and preventing access to resources they had shared with settlers for hundreds of years.

It was 2008, and through three different interviews, neither the organizers nor I ever discussed the role or approval of Indigenous Nations for this land-based project.

Treaty 4 is the only Numbered Treaty in Canada with a visual interpretation as a corresponding record of the Crown's agreements with Cree, Saulteaux, and Assiniboine Nations. The visual document was made by Chief Paskwa of the Pasqua First Nation nine years after signing Treaty 4, who wanted his interpretation of the treaty—and its failings—to be given to the Queen, but the Englishman to whom he entrusted his paper ended up framing it as a souvenir that stayed in his family's personal collection until 2000, when his descendants auctioned it off to the highest bidder.

Saskatchewan's horizons are vast. The sun blazes and the wind whistles through the brightest, clearest light across golden fields and crisp blue skies. Saskatchewan is also one of the most deeply segregated provinces when it comes to Indigenous and settler rights, from the basic necessities to the court of law. When the not-guilty verdict was announced in the death of a young Indigenous man in 2018, leaders and individuals from across the nations stood up and grieved. Some settlers mourned, but others gloated that he got what he deserved. He was a twenty-two-year-old out joyriding with his girlfriend and their friends. He lived on the land of his ancestors and was a member of the Cree Red Pheasant First Nation, a band just south of North Battleford, in Treaty 6 territory. Like many bored and listless young people in the Prairies, they had allegedly shared a few drinks and gone swimming. Afterwards, they drove toward home on secondary roads before blowing a tire.

Donna has done the exact same thing. I have, too. But neither of us nor our predominantly white friends have ever been shot at, even if trespassing across private property. The white farmer said he thought they were thieves in his yard, so he fired his handgun at point-blank range, killing the young man, who had never left his car. The shooter then went back inside his house and drank coffee with his wife until the RCMP came—RCMP who, for weeks, treated the victim's grieving friends and family like criminals. The slain young man was put on trial, and late on a Friday evening, after only two days of deliberation, an all-white jury in North Battleford found the white farmer not guilty of manslaughter.

Donna watched, silently at first, as her extended family, her old friends, past co-workers, and former neighbours shared amongst themselves on public social forums that a man has the right to protect his property, and that race has nothing to do with the law. She felt her obligation as a white settler was to sit in the discomfort and sift through all of the ill-informed and factually incorrect re-sponses made by her people before responding herself. Even though she was outnumbered, she still had to say something.

Growing up in Moose Jaw in the eighties and nineties, Donna and her older sister rocked some amazing looks in their old family photos. Over the years, she showed them to me without shame or pride. She and her sister were pale as ghosts, with dark hair and dark eyes, but that was the norm back then. In a few of the photos, her adopted siblings, one girl and one boy, joined them for awkward portraits. While they shared familial resemblances in their dark hair and kitchen-sink haircuts, they did not share Donna's bone-white pallor.

Even as a child, Donna had sensed that something was off. As an adult, she became aware that her family fully participated in violent dynamics with her adopted Indigenous siblings. She kept looking back, trying to come to terms with what had happened inside her own family. Do children know they are receiving preferential treatment? Or do they only notice when they experience unfairness first-hand? Her adopted sister eventually ran away, and her adopted brother went to live with their dad after the divorce. Then he ran away, too. Donna, meanwhile, grew up doing what you did in Saskatchewan: driving to the farm, dating hockey players, learning to shotgun a beer, and deciding between leaving or staying as per family tradition.

Since becoming a parent herself, Donna has tried reconnecting with her adopted siblings. More than twenty years have passed, and she knows in advance that they may want nothing to do with her. She has learned more about Canada's child welfare system, including its past and ongoing protocols to forcibly remove Indigenous children from their communities. Her sister, Carol, has also built a family of her own, and while not exactly icy, she's not been open when messaging back and forth with Donna about their lives. Carol has taken a long road back toward reconnecting with her birth family, and Donna can only affirm to her how fucked-up their overlapping childhoods had been. When Donna mentions she has two boys of her own now, she can see Carol is genuinely happy for her. She reminds Donna to take lots of pictures of them at this age. Donna both really appreciates this advice and is absolutely wrecked by it. Their brother, James, has been incarcerated off and on for decades. Donna has searched for his whereabouts for years, but no one in her immediate family cares. She feels concern. Guilt. Shame. She knows her experiences are secondary to what has happened. His personhood goes largely unacknowledged by her family, who want nothing to do with that chapter in their lives. As hard-working, down-to-earth people, they will never admit to holding prejudice against any Indigenous person, even when they are family.

On our last trip together in Saskatchewan, Donna and I drove through Saskatoon to have breakfast with one of her oldest friends. Married with kids—one at school and one on the way—it was a short catch-up where nothing new was said, merely old memories rehashed with laughs. I felt out of place but smiled when they laughed, ate what they ate, and asked the ages of the children. Afterwards, Donna wanted to drive around a bit more, to go over the city's bridges that had earned Saskatoon the nickname as the Venice of the Prairies. I have also heard it called the Paris of the Prairies, but both are equally absurd. Applying ill-fitting European parameters onto these freshwater grasslands is to be blind to everything that is already there. I have more recently heard Saskatchewan's racial segregation and systematic discrimination described as the Johannesburg of Canada, but South Africa's white minority leaders had actually borrowed a page from Canada's residential school system in establishing their apartheid.

As we drove out past the South Saskatchewan heading east toward the sun, we stopped the car to take a better look at all that was familiar and past. Donna choked up for a minute before quickly apologizing. Standing by the side of the road as the grass billowed across the fields and the morning sun stretched across the horizon, I have to assume that this is what Canadians do when they finally feel and see things they cannot find the words for.

The Cairn

Between 2007 and 2011, I drove thousands of kilometres between Alberta, Saskatchewan, and Manitoba, criss-crossing between Treaty 1 through 8 territories. I was researching for a group exhibition that spoke to my experience of the Plains, a narrative that neither romanticized the Prairies nor followed the region's mid-twentieth-century art history as a Modernist haven. Both of these established narratives reiterated a specific logic, where the land, the wind, and everything in between had to be claimed and mastered before it could enter the realm of the nation-state's comprehension. Having spent the majority of my life between two British colonies, I had yet to understand the complexities of settlers and colonization. Instinctively, because Canadian history books and their authors had seemed inadequate for most of my life, I searched for the role that women played in homesteading this region. Extending this perspective into contemporary art, I brought together twelve female artists from the three prairie provinces who, more or less, had never heard of each other.

The majority of artists in the exhibition *They Made a Day Be a Day Here* had roots in Manitoba, predominantly Winnipeg. Most provinces have at least two major cities competing against each other for provincial resources and university subsidies, but Winnipeg had the lion's share all to herself. Brandon came in a distant second, at almost a tenth of Winnipeg's population. I had only visited Brandon once, and that felt enough. Brief and extended visits to Treaty 1 would be entirely consumed by activities in Winnipeg, whose food scene has always been one of my favourites in the country. As decades of racist immigration policy shaped where and when "undesirable" immigrants could settle after Confederation, large influxes of racialized immigrants began settling all over the Prairies. While Anglo-Saxon British immigrants were understood as the "desirable" immigrants the country needed to settle the nation's urban centres, then Minister of the Interior Clifford Sifton pushed ahead an open-door immigration policy encouraging minority European groups like Ukrainians, Hungarians, Mennonites, and Doukhobors to settle and farm the land across the Prairies. Large waves of immigration ended up coming from everywhere, from Iceland to India, and more recently, Winnipeg has become home to the largest population of Filipinos per capita in the country. At one point, the greater region of Winnipeg was home to the largest concentration of multilingual newspapers, running upwards of 140 ethnic dailies serving Yiddish to Polish to Vietnamese readers. When I say Winnipeg is my favorite Canadian city, I'm not saying it's perfect. Not by a long shot. I am, however, stricken to my core by the city's countless contradictions and multiplicities. It's trying to be an honest place, and that's enough for me.

For most of my visits through the 2000s, and certainly before, the city carried a rough and tough reputation where racism and poverty had nowhere to hide. It's a place where you could see a guy heavily bleeding on a city bus because he's been stabbed and can't afford to call an ambulance or even take a cab to the hospital. I have seen teenage moms with fresh black eyes, bruises on their arms, weighed down by kids being accosted by surly, impatient public servants who have seen it all before. Those struck hardest by poverty and violence were almost always Indigenous children, women, and men, and nobody bats an eye. Just business as usual along the Red River.

Winnipeg and Edmonton used to compete for the title of "murder city capital of Canada." I had always talked about doing a show with the title *Murder City* with Winnipeg artist and curator Shawna Dempsey, but nothing ever materialized. Back in 2008 or 2009, we never considered that Winnipeg and Edmonton had the two highest urban populations of First Nations and Métis peoples in the country. We never consciously connected the statistics of violence in our respective cities' populations to the breakdown of the systems holding together the myth of Canada. Our idea was a failure from the very beginning, but it gave us enough reason to keep talking.

When I came through Winnipeg in the summer of 2017,

after a three-year absence, I noticed a slight difference in the air. In the district of Fort Rouge, Anishinaabe activist and public broadcaster Wab Kinew was now the district's MLA and leader of the Manitoba New Democratic Party. For the first time ever in the province's history, almost a third of the NDP MLAs in Manitoba were of Indigenous heritage. During my first time visiting Winnipeg, I remembered having to sidestep a pool of blood on the sidewalk on a search for food after dark. Ten years later, on the very same strip, high-end bistros and organic food stores now lined the street. Somethings change, but most of the time, that change is only beneficial for a limited number of people.

They say nostalgia is a dangerous thing. This is especially true for those with no future. Nostalgia exists within the confines of how good something used to be, be it a place, a relationship, or a meal. But was it ever really that good? The Prairies, and Winnipeg specifically, creates in me nostalgia for a life that was never mine.

On my last full day in Winnipeg, Shawna and her girlfriend Wanda pick me up for a whirlwind tour of eats and errands. Wanda met Shawna at a Pride event in Thompson, Manitoba, where she was playing with her band, and where Shawna, with an infallible sense of direction, wandered through a random door and into the backstage area. Three years later, they picked me up at Sarah's house so they could ogle their dream house next door. The place was tucked into a corner lot backing onto the Assiniboine; I had never noticed how close I was staying to the river. On the way to Winnipeg, I read in my inflight magazine that the river system is the best way to travel through cities like Winnipeg, Ottawa, Quebec City, and Edmonton. Considering that these cities were built around active fur-trade routes between Indigenous Nations and Europeans, routes that developed over hundreds of years, it's a wonder that the rivers remain so underused. It's like ignoring a house's central staircase, opting instead to use the scaffolding outside to get up and down all day.

As the three of us floated down the Assiniboine on a waterbus tour, Shawna pointed out the back lot of her and Wanda's dream house. We also saw three young deer roaming through the bush, and the beginnings of a beaver dam. When the tour was over, I stood along the riverbank where the Assiniboine and Red Rivers met. The water was as murky as mud in the Assiniboine, but slightly more green in the Red. Their two streams merged with effortless force, each remaining distinct.

We had begun the day with the first of many meals. This is what we did best together. The first time we went for coffee, Shawna ordered half a pound of shaved prosciutto alongside a custard-filled Long John from an Italian bakery in Edmonton. That meal set a tone. On this sunny day in Winnipeg, the three of us dug into some fried salami and smoked tongue sandwiches at Sherbrook Street Delicatessen. Shawna ordered her tongue with a smear of liver pate, and I doubled my sandwich fillings. With my first bite, I immediately regretted my gristly choice. I remembered the tongue as melt-in-your-mouth, but memories often taste better when left behind.

Shawna has a long itinerary planned for the day, and after lunch we drive over to Neechi Commons, an Indigenous-run space that functions as a grocery store, restaurant, art gallery, and community centre. Neechi Commons is where Anishinaabe artist Rebecca Belmore worked on her bead and ceramic commission for the Canadian Museum for Human Rights. I think about going to this museum, but I never do. The CMHR has been significant for many Jewish settlers in this country, but controversy has plagued the project from the beginning over what was and wasn't going to be acknowledged inside its walls. The building had been a dream project of the Aspers, once major newsprint publishers in Canada, who wanted to build a Canadian museum to commemorate Holocaust survivors. Before its doors even opened to the public in 2013, the museum's refusal to use the word *genocide* in relation to Canada's treatment of Indigenous Peoples had marred its reputation; in a press statement, its CEO said it was not the role of the museum to declare what constitutes genocide. Considering the museum sits at the mouth of where the Assiniboine and Red Rivers meet, on the site of the founding of Canada by way of the bloodshed of the Red River settlements, people were rightfully offended.

In an interview with *Canadian Art*, Belmore said she was interested in making a blanket composed of individual beads, where each bead was made from clay dug up from the Red River Valley. Each bead reveals the tactile imprints of the many different hands that have worked on its surface over the years at Neechi Commons. Titled *Trace*, the work is a tangible accumulation and embodied reminder of how we shape this land when we work together.

In the places we end up living, where we find ourselves out of need and circumstance, we live with one another. Sometimes we live next to those who have stolen from us, and sometimes we live next to those we have stolen from. Let us not erase each other further.

It has been quipped to me that the Canadian Museum for Human Rights is a whole lot of building for a website. I would rather visit the grocery store at Neechi Commons, but we arrive half an hour before they open. Shawna is visibly disappointed as the day is packed and we shan't be waiting around in this empty parking lot. I don't know Wanda very well, but I get a sense that she's uncomfortable. Maybe it was the fried salami talking, but something changed when we drove into the North End. Only later do I learn that Wanda's relative had just been stabbed that weekend on Main Street. He didn't survive. Wanda wasn't uncomfortable. She had a heavy heart.

From the back seat of Wanda's car, I hear bits and pieces of their conversation, about how their family histories are intertwined. They clarify that their families did not directly know one another, but that Wanda's people, the Swampy Cree, signed Treaty 5 in 1875 in Norway House on her mother's side and in 1876 in the Pas on her father's side. Treaty signings were taken seriously by Indigenous Nations, and it is almost certain Wanda's great-great-great-grandparents would have been present. Shawna's great-grandfather, Joseph Dempsey, the last to flee from Ireland's famine, arrived in Treaty 1 territory in 1877. For the first year, he worked manual labour, digging out basements in Winnipeg by shovel. In 1878, he walked over

150 kilometres to Treaty 5 territory, to lay claim to 320 acres of land near present-day Carberry for a twenty-dollar registration fee. It would be the first year that land in that region was made available to settlers for the price of farming the soil, which, to the newly formed country of Canada, outweighed the Royal Proclamation's promises to leave Indigenous Nations and land alone with the exception of negotiating fair and legal treaties. Treaty 5 made it possible for Shawna's great-grandfather to take "free" land and farm it at the dispossession of Indigenous sovereignty. In this way, the stories of Shawna's and Wanda's families were linked.

With mnemonic directions from Shawna, Wanda drives them outside the city limits and west on Highway 1. Driving past Headingley, Wanda tells her passengers that for every fifteen wooden posts on these straight and narrow highways, the distance spanned amounts to a kilometre, or nineteen posts to a mile. Standard measurement elsewhere is forty posts to a mile, but Manitoba has always been different.

We pull over on the side of an unassuming stretch of road to get a closer look at what appears at first to be a small stack of stones, like a tomb. A small cairn has been erected to commemorate the Dominion's first stake of measuring land in 1871, which opened the floodgates for settlement and expansion. Its significance as a measuring system, otherwise known as the land survey, was the key mechanism in parcelling out the Prairies for non-Indigenous settlement. When Louis Riel famously put his foot on the surveyor's chain in 1869, his gesture was considered the first step in the Red River Resistance. With the first stake planted, he knew it was the beginning of the end. The cairn's plaque flatly reads:

> *The first marker of the Dominion Lands Survey was placed 10 July, 1871, on the Principal Meridian, about half a mile south of this site. The system then inaugurated by Lieutenant Colonel J. S. Dennis, Surveyor-General, extends across the prairies and to the Pacific coast, embracing more than 200 million acres of surveyed lands in Manitoba, Saskatchewan, Alberta, and parts of British Columbia.*

To date, Indigenous lands south of the 60th parallel add up to less than one-half of one per cent of Canada's land mass. Because of the unique scrip system put into place, Métis in Manitoba are still fighting for their rightful use of land that had been negotiated, stolen, sold unwillingly, and then fraudulently acquired by newcomers. By 1812, the Dominion needed settlers to defend the Crown from the United States, and land was surveyed and given to incoming waves of European immigrants looking to survive and prosper. Settlers flooded westward and systematic protocols to contain and eradicate Indigenous communities became a state department. Shawna and Wanda have come out here before. This cairn is a monument to the founding of Manitoba and the settlement of Canada. Its history lives inside all of us.

Having already been to Louis Riel's grave in St. Boniface

at different points in each of our lives, we instead drive to his house, located along the Red River. Riel's wife and kids had lived in the house for a time when they had nowhere else to go, but we learned Riel himself never actually lived there. This house was designated a national historic site ninety-four years after the Canadian government hanged Riel for treason. It was where his body was laid out for over 10,000 people to pay their final respects. Parks Canada now cares for this property frozen macabrely in time, with a full garden and teenagers dressed up in period costumes to emulate the year following Riel's execution in Regina. Sugarcoated in all of the didactic panels is how Canada was founded on the settlement of the west, joining Upper and Lower Canada to the vast tracts of resource-rich country, which also meant they had to get through the Red River Valley by signing the Manitoba Act of 1870 with its list of rights to protect Métis land and people. To this day, these rights have never been fully honoured by the Canadian government.

In year 150 of this country's confederation, I overheard questionable facts being doled out to a white man with a big camera by a white teenager in a bonnet. A small rotting buffalo hide was hanging along the fence at the Riel home, presumably to make the grounds more authentic to non-Indigenous visitors. It was a muggy day, and the costumed teenagers in their layers of wool stood cooling themselves in the shade, leaving no one tending the gift basket of handmade Métis sashes baking in the sun. I wandered out past the yard, following Shawna into the garden to pick raspberries in the last of the afternoon heat.

The Red River lots were lush and fertile farming lands, designed after the narrow French-Canadian river-lot style with individualized access to water, making each Métis farm home self-sustaining.

As the day waned and with the raspberries whetting our appetites once again, Shawna's last stop for us was at the Forks for an early dinner and an impromptu boat ride. It was a Sunday, so children ran wild and families aired out, parents and grandparents alike exhausted but happy. The three of us tucked into our piping-hot fried pickerel and chips, and Shawna recalled that the last time she and Wanda ate at Fergies was during Winnipeg Pride. They had met Riley, a two-spirited man who happily accepted the invitation from two strangers to join them at their dinner table. The only seat left in the room was for Riley. Digging into her mound of salted and vinegared chips on fake newsprint, Wanda fondly recalled meeting Riley, who came down every year for Pride. After collecting enough empties, he would treat himself to a serving of fish and chips from Fergies. He said that doing so made him taste home, and everyone needs a sense of home. Wanda recalled that, as he said this, the two of them shared a look, giving each other a nod of acknowledgement, and both cracking the smallest smiles.

Choke

Spending the better part of 2011 in the northeast of Scot-land, in a tiny, violent town, I wake up one cold, drizzling morning flooded with images of a riot happening half a world away. West Georgia Street had been taken over from Seymour Street down. Cars had been lit on fire and store-fronts completely smashed in. Bodies and heads had been painted blue and white, marching alongside jerseys that matched those distorted, jubilant faces. I could see flashes of a modern-day Roman Coliseum set in the background. Only in chaos did that architecture finally feel fitting.

Predictably, the media and the good people of Vancouver blamed their second modern-day hockey riot on a handful of hooligans. In a city with an already long history of civic riots, those to blame always came from elsewhere. These angry fans were most likely, surely, from the outlying areas of Surrey, or maybe even Richmond. The day after the riot, thousands of *real* Vancouverites reportedly flooded the streets with brooms in hand, ready to clean up the debris and wipe clean the city's pristine image of itself. After the first hockey riot in 1994, when the New York Rangers defeated the Canucks, then-mayor Philip Owen was quoted as describing the riot as a symptom of the "deep social problems across the country." In 2011, while I watched the city burn itself down after the Boston Bruins swept the Canucks, Mayor Gregor Robertson proclaimed, "Vancouver is a world-class city," and that such violence "is embarrassing and shameful to see."

The lesson, and the attitude, is that no matter what happens here, the problem is never Vancouver's fault.

My mother, Cho Kei—or Maggie, as her friends in Canada now call her—lives alone in a condo tower just a few blocks away from where the riot occurred. Speaking over Skype, she described the riot as being very noisy, and that, simply, "those people" were mad and insane. Whenever she would describe someone as having gone mad, the translation from Mandarin to English conjured up images of a person who has eaten too much, to the point of choking. This person, being fulfilled, and with nothing better to do, has gone stark raving mad. In Mandarin, the inflection for *insane* also sounds a lot like the inflection for *wind*, as in *those people are now in the wind*. For a woman who has lived through the rise and reign of Mao, and who independently moved her three children across the Pacific Ocean to get farther away from China's Communist government, those fulfilled people in the wind did not bother her so much.
But she knew she might bother them a touch.

Walking her rescue dog, Sunshine—a snaggle-toothed Lhasa Apso—twice a day along the False Creek seawall, my mother makes a point of telling entitled and inquiring busybodies that she has lived in Canada for thirty years. She doesn't want any of these nosy strangers to mistake her for one of those new Chinese immigrants, the so-called "Beijing billionaires" who are publicly and privately blamed across Vancouver for the bloated housing market, which is now unattainable for the average Canadian. She counts herself as lucky for getting into the condo market before it skyrocketed, knowing there was no way she could afford to stay as a separated retiree living off a modest old-age pension.

During early-morning grocery-shopping trips via the #23 bus, Cho Kei would watch as entire blocks started coming down and condos started shooting up along Main Street and East Georgia. She could not understand why anyone would choose to live in Chinatown if they didn't have to. *Why would anyone choose to live in a poor neighbourhood?* she asked me once, confused, annoyed, and perhaps unaware of the historical arc from racial ghettoization to its inevitable collision with artistic ambitions, gentrification, and development potential.

Between 2011 and 2014, I saw a lot of art shows about precarious labour and gentrification. Moving to Vancouver after a half-year stint in the UK, I had been well-accustomed to the generously state-funded frameworks of art and art workers toiling away in a constant rate of precarity, which in and of itself perpetuates a precarious industrial complex all its own. Most of these ironic exhibitions occurred in galleries that had moved into Chinatown, or in those situated below single room occupancies or in pop-up spaces in the Downtown Eastside. I often walked in the drizzling rain from one show to another, in small, loose groups of people visiting from out of town or who were back in town for a short stint. We would trek up and down Main Street or Hastings, trying to end the night down the hill, if possible. The evening streets were always darker in Vancouver than in any other city, the paved roads slick with faint amber dew. The people I walked with would change from week to week. Never knowing any one of them too well, I generally found people in Vancouver to be socially aloof, but intellectually demanding and emotionally withholding. Even if I had met the same person three or four times, it would be a strange encounter if I was to say hello.

Social spaces were detached from their urban fabric, sitting invisible to those who had not been led in through darkened entranceways, back alleys, and shuttered front windows into the packed humdrum of artist-run speakeasies. Walking by their storefronts in the daytime, I would often pause for a second to see if this was in fact where I had been the night before. For artists who could afford to live in this city, was exclusivity a cherished prize for surviving?

I would overhear on a constant rotation:

Entire blocks of mansions are being bought up by the Chinese, who just let them sit empty in West Vancouver. Houses are being flipped by them, six, seven times in the span of weeks, from seller to final buyer. These illegal Chinese businessmen are dumping their stolen equity into Vancouver real estate, laundering their dirty money in our housing market!

...

But remember how unfair Vancouver has been to Asians "in the past." The Chinese head tax, their treatment on the railway. The formation by union workers of an Asiatic Exclusion League, who chanted "White Power" as they walked through the streets of Chinatown. We have to save Chinatown, for historical reasons. We can't blame Chinese foreign investment, because we can't be seen as scapegoating them again.

I hear all sides of the housing crisis, and how it relates to foreign investment. I hear it almost always anecdotally. Intergenerational guilt and shame co-mingling with continual invisible entitlement rendering an impotent desire to right to white all that has been passed.

The task of holding class-based differences across race seemed impossible for the right and left to hold.

In a city littered with draconian bylaws, the artist-run speakeasy was something, anything, to do at night. Long serious conversations took place in such cafés or studios-turned-bars. Over bitters-infused cocktails and fresh-squeezed orange juice, skinny bodies pressed closer together to talk at length about neo-liberalism. On the rare occasion a dance party started, groups of sullen faces could still be seen huddled in dark corners, sharing lucid critiques of late capitalism, negativity, and revolution. These conversations carried over into dinner parties, birthday parties, and outdoor gatherings, where I always felt pulled into performing rather than relaxing. One evening, after another failed dance party at the Astoria, a small group of acquaintances—mostly academic poets and myself—ended up in the backyard of a young self-identified socialist. The conversation was already circular, posturing with no power, before the host started making a show for the small, drunken crowd by reading aloud the youthful poetry of Mao Zedong. I put my drink down and turned to the host. *What do you think you're doing?* I asked this pale, skinny boy. *Do you know what kind of man he was?* I sneered the words, unable to hide anything. *Do you know who you're actually reading?* The socialist boy with brown hair and brown eyes kept reading Mao's poems aloud. He continued steadily even after I erupted into a *What kind of fucking ignorant idiot would even read this shit?* monologue. One of the senior poets laughed at my profanity from either nerves or ennui. Another boy, who was studying at Simon Fraser University, made an intellectual observation about Orientalism, and everyone slowly went inside.

A few weeks later, at a panel on decolonization, the skinny boy with the serious expression comes up to me sheepishly to say he was just joking around about Mao. I don't respond and start to actively freeze him out of conversations. Mutual friends notice my animosity toward him, and when they hear what happened, they enthusiastically tell me how he is actually really nice, how he was raised by a single mom and fights for affordable housing. Exasperation lingers in their voices when they defend him, or those like him, who are nice and actively erase me.

"We are not yet strong enough to assimilate races so alien from us in their habits. We are afraid that they would swamp our civilization such as it is."
—Editorial, Nanaimo *Free Press*, May 29, 1914

"Perhaps we should seriously consider whether we can continue to admit so many immigrants...maybe we should make it less desirable for people to migrate to Vancouver from other areas of Canada by making it more attractive for them to remain where they are."
—Former BC premier and then-alderman Mike Harcourt, *The Housing Crisis*, 1970

"So you can now enjoy the 'privilege' of being marginalized in the community your forefathers built, have neighbours who refuse to speak your language, and not be able to afford a home!"
—anonymous flyers distributed across Richmond, BC, 2016

The first time I heard anyone tell another person they should go back to where they supposedly came from was on a bus in Edmonton. I was twelve years old and riding the hour and a half from my elementary school in the north end to my new house in the west end. I had moved five times in six years and was not moving schools again with two months left in grade school. My mother reluctantly drove me across town every morning with the deal that I would take the three buses back home or to her flower shop every day straight after school. It was a deal that brokered my transition into independence.

On one of these journeys, as I hurtled down 101 Street on a half-empty bus, I sat watching for the shiny bunting hanging over the used-car lots north of downtown—a sign that we were leaving the suburbs. I remembered how glaring the bunting could be under the prairie sun, and how those sharp triangles of reflected light never stopped sparkling despite their depressing surroundings. I had been trying not to stare too much at the window, particularly the faces in front of it, as I was taught it was rude to stare at strangers, but I was distracted by the warbling voice of a man hoarsely talking to someone who was not responding. He was making one-sided chatter, and from his intonations I wondered if he was really tired or just drunk. He had the rough complexion of somebody over twenty but under fifty, with a labourer's tan. No one intervened until the young Asian woman he was sitting next to broke down into tears. When she wasn't receptive to his questions, he told her she should just go back to China. He tried to qualify to the half-empty bus that if she wasn't going to talk to a nice Canadian guy like him, she should just go back home. Another man told him to get off the bus, which he did, when his stop came up. At the time, I wondered if this was true, that to fit into this country I would have to let "real" Canadians talk to me. By the time I got off the bus, the woman was still sitting there, sobbing quietly. Even at twelve years old, I felt a shame rising in me, at my inability to speak up, and in realizing that I was also vulnerable to this threat of being told to return to a place to which I no longer belonged.

It would take years for me to realize that the string of white men and women who proudly claimed their Canadian roots and values were also not from this country. Their fervour was infectious and reinforced through every grand narrative I would hear for years to come. In Vancouver specifically, the sense of who belonged and who didn't took on a rampant tone, and, since its earliest incarnation as Saltwater City, there has always been hostility between whites, who took everything they laid their eyes on, and everybody else, who were consistently pushed out—that is, if they were allowed into the country at all.

My mother's neighbourhood friends in Vancouver are all elderly Chinese women, some of whom speak fluent Mandarin or Cantonese, or have spoken only English their entire lives. They come from Taiwan, Calgary, Hong Kong, Thailand, and the Republic of Mauritius. In their retirement, they busied themselves by walking their small dogs twice a day along the False Creek Seawall. All of them have been individually told over the years by complete strangers—always white men and women—to go back to China. They would be told off because they were overheard speaking to each other in foreign tones, because they were sitting in a public spot the white people had wanted to sit in, or because they had decided to stay and live their lives. My mother has also been told by a stranger to go back to China, and without a pause she told him that *he* should go. She laughed a dirty little laugh when recounting the story to me. *These white people*, she said shaking her head, *they have eaten too much. They are choking themselves.*

Witness

Shortly after moving to Vancouver in 2011, I learned that most left-leaning politics, from academia to activism, held a great amount of cultural cachet. The only identities on trend at that time were anti-neo-liberalism and Indigenous allyship. Everything in between was a blur, a nonentity devoid of specificity and nuance. You were either for or against something or someone until it professionally suited you to believe and behave in the complete opposite manner. I had come from the Prairies, where if someone said they would meet you at a spot in six months' time, they would be there. No day-of check-ins to confirm time and place. No email reminders necessary. Most importantly, no rain checks ever. In Vancouver, though, I could never get a sense of where people stood on anything. It was hard enough for peers to keep to scheduled meetings. Day-of reminders always had to be sent, and last-minute rain checks were more common than not. I found the lack of will to commit to any single position, even a specific time and place, was hard won. I learned to stop taking it personally, as it was common behaviour across the board—a mix of snobbery clouded with crippling self-consciousness undertoned every potential social encounter. Group hangouts were easier to mitigate, but the dynamics were the same, slightly diffused and easier to slip away from.

I was lost amongst the lost. It took several awkward encounters before I fully understood what "TRC" even stood for. Peers were not generous with information, especially if it meant they could hold some unnamed power over one another. Most of those who had begun dropping TRC into conversations were dropping it like a new band—like, "Are you going to go to the TRC when it comes to town?" or, "I don't know how I feel about the TRC." I had no idea what I thought or felt. Most settlers didn't seem to either, but I can say now for certain: the Truth and Reconciliation Commission wasn't and isn't for any non-Indigenous person to banter about as their ill-informed nebulous opinion. Created as one of several concrete outcomes from the Indian Residential Schools Settlement Agreement, the Truth and Reconciliation Commission was tasked to collect and preserve the stories of survivors. Modelled after South Africa's Truth and Reconciliation Commission, which assembled after apartheid had officially ended in 1994, the model has been used by various nations to document their own human rights violations. As a bureaucratic humanitarian structure, its primary aim aspires to record the experiences of those involved in cases such as human rights violations and cultural genocide, with the goal of restorative healing for survivors and perpetrators alike. Looking at the outcome so far of Canada's TRC, the emphasis has been overwhelmingly on survivor trauma, a pain that settlers have long been desensitized to and can digest with their morning tea. There is a sentiment that the past is the past and people just need to move on from it, but this opinion is always heard from the most ensconced position of comfort and power. They do not realize that their refusal to change and adapt is the barrier to healing, to justice, and to moving on.

The process of learning what has happened, let alone reconciling, feels far from complete. I can only speak for myself as a first-generation settler who has spent most of my life trying to assimilate into a colonial nation. This process of shifting my world views away from the linear and binary world of Eurocentricism has been more of a letting go and a returning to thought patterns and language formations that I have suppressed long ago. From simply trying to fit in as the new kid in what was always a majority-white student body, to the structures of whiteness, including academia, corporate culture, and non-profit culture, I have always had to choose between naming myself within the silo of diversity or having the privilege of s(l)iding into whiteness as default.

In this moment in time, I have never witnessed so much discussion on the subject of race and inequality across this country. I want to believe this is a positive thing, despite the capitalization of trauma by and for whiteness that we as audiences are currently expected to applaud. Even in the process of writing this manuscript, I am wary of performing pain for a hungry yet apathetic market.

Beyond the internalized logics of self-doubt, where growing up through the perceived safety and success of whiteness was the only desirable normalcy by my concerned mother for her children, the willful ignorance of colonial trauma against Indigenous Nations and peoples remains an ongoing violence perpetuated by settler immigrants. To the limits of my knowledge, residential-school survivor stories only began being publicly shared— at least beyond quiet words or unspoken feelings with non-Indigenous people—in the 1990s. The last residential school in Canada did not close until 1996, the same year the Royal Commission on Aboriginal Peoples would be released, with its conclusive summary: *The main policy direction, pursued for more than 150 years, first by colonial then by Canadian governments, has been wrong.*

Canada separated children from their parents, sending them to residential schools. It was done not to educate them, but primarily to break their link to their culture and identity. In justifying the government's residential school policy, Canada's first prime minister, Sir John A. Macdonald, told the House of Commons in 1883:

> *When the school is on the reserve the child lives with its parents, who are savages; he is surround-ed by savages, and though he may learn to read and write his habits, and training and mode of thought are Indian. He is simply a savage who can read and write. It has been strongly pressed on myself, as the head of the Department, that Indian children should be withdrawn as much as*

possible from the parental influence, and the only
way to do that would be to put them in central
training industrial schools where they will acquire
the habits and modes of thought of white men.
(from *Honouring the Truth, Reconciling for the*
Future, 2015)

From the West End, I had taken two buses, the 19 and
then the 16, east toward the Pacific National Exhibition
grounds, where the summer fair happened every year. I
had never been to Hastings Park before. Thousands of
people were already gathered there that morning, and the
smell of fire and sage thickened the air. I made my way
inside the Pacific Coliseum as bodies moved in every direction, in neither a rush nor a relaxed pace. I climbed up
as far as the bleachers would go and took an empty seat.
Politicians were still speaking onstage, so I knew I hadn't
missed anything. When the first Elder spoke, the cameras
were still flashing and the blazers flanking on either side
dabbed their eyes. I don't remember what happened next.
Hours ticked by. A stream of voices spoke. Some were
young, but most had decades of repression to shed. My
awareness of violent assimilation processes perpetrated
by the government of Canada was almost nil before 2011.
I had not heard the phrase *intergenerational trauma* until
that day. These words made true something I had never
understood before. In the late afternoon, I left the Coliseum to walk because my body needed to move. It was
raining. I wandered past the booths and the lake. Tempo-
rary exhibitions were installed everywhere and drumming
could still be heard from a not-so-far-off distance. I hadn't

known that day about the livestock barns on the PNE grounds, where over 8,000 citizens of Japanese descent were forcibly held in the 1940s, penned like animals before being forced into labour farms and interment camps in the name of national security. In total, over 20,000 people, a majority of them born in British Columbia, were rounded up. Their personal assets liquidated to offset the operating costs of their own internment. I didn't know much about the history of this country at all.

A few weeks prior, I had taken the 99 bus out to UBC, rumbling my elbows against the stranger sitting beside me. I had skipped the opening at the Morris and Helen Belkin Art Gallery, preferring to not see the show with lots of other bodies milling around, cracker crumbs spitting out of their open mouths and sticky fingers reaching for another piece of fruit or cheese. I didn't want to see any of it or be seen at any of it; I just wanted to see the work, and openings are never opportunities to see work.

Works from the exhibition by Lisa Jackson and Skeena Reece would linger in my mind. A still from Jackson's short film *Savage* was used as publicity for the exhibition: a green-faced child more ghoul than girl leered forward, elbows out, ready to pounce from behind her small wooden desk. The publicity shot looked like a movie poster for a new horror film, and that was likely the point.

In the work by Reece, a maternal figure haunts the screen. She looks back at us, inconsolable from the loss of her missing children. She appears lost to the world in her mourning. I remembered it was silent in the gallery and I began to understand something else for the first time. I would and could never fully understand the specificity of pain caused by residential schools and the damage done to those who were taken and those who were left behind. At best, I could witness the survivors, and listen to what Elders had been asking when they asked you to try and imagine living in a community where there are no children.

The artist talk took place in the back corner of the gallery, with a few rows of chairs shaped into a crescent moon and the speaker in the centre. It was a small crowd, and the talk, along with the dynamics in the room, saw a largely white-settler audience passively watching an Inuk artist, the speaker, relive his colonial trauma. When tears started falling down his face, the other artist from the exhibition was the only person to get up and put her arms around him. The gallery staff, as well as all the audience members, sat there looking increasingly uncomfortable as we gazed down at the space between our feet. I could only look around the room at the collective inaction, frozen in my own passivity.

Prior to seeing the show, I had heard lots of good things about the exhibition, *Witnesses: Art and Canada's Indian Residential Schools*, but it was hard to take such accolades seriously when everything was always being hyped as a "must-see." I thought the show could very well be great, but wished there was support for a spectrum of criticism and responses—especially around identity-based exhibitions. Art magazines, which are predominantly run by white editors and publishers, don't have a lot of guts when it comes to talking about racial nuance. They see "identity-based" anything and simply applaud and rejoice. I continue to think this pandering actually does everyone a disservice, but I know my opinions remain in the minority.

I had stopped writing for art publications after years as a full-time freelance art critic. The hustle no longer suited the rhythms of how I wanted to experience art or life. Sound bites and hot takes cannot hold all that remains invisible and present in the world. Complexities do not need another simplified breakdown. Criticality is harder to market, often reserved for academics with specialized language, but criticality is actually the moment when we begin to be a little more honest with ourselves and each other.

The multicultural myth of Canada has always been undermined by the government's assimilation of and genocidal policies toward Indigenous Nations. Difference against whiteness has never been easily embraced, not for Indigenous Nations, early POC settlers, or Black migrants. More often than not, difference has been so effortlessly met with state violence turned law turned status quo. Diversity works only for whiteness, for those who are happy to benevolently oversee and control diversity in all its frivolous forms, but who will immediately enforce the power of their laws the moment difference seeks actual power.

As 2017 reached its frenzied pinnacle with simultaneous over-the-top celebrations and scathing critiques of 150 years of Canada as a colonial nation, there followed a plethora of artistic output that spoke to a collective unknowing by whiteness: countless theatrical productions, literary essays, and gallery exhibitions flooded out, acknowledging the tragedies and violence of colonization and white supremacy. One year later, it was almost back to business as usual. Whiteness could relax again. But during that pinnacle arc, the concluding summary to these festivities was how each project reached some cathartic place, admitting: *We didn't know.*

We didn't know that so many children suffered horrific abuses We didn't know they killed all of their hunting sled dogs We didn't know families were broken inside out We didn't know about ongoing trauma We didn't know about mental illnesses We didn't know this land wasn't ours for the taking We didn't know youth suicide was tearing communities apart We didn't know there wasn't adequate housing We didn't know our justice system was broken We didn't know what was considered racist We didn't know

But now we do Now we do know We know Some of us knew We know now

We All Know We Knew.

The Tour

The bus had stopped again, this time in a parking lot on Treaty Trail. We had started the day at Peggy's Cove at the crack of dawn with a heavy, salt-laden breakfast at the top of the hill and were now on the clock to hit New Glasgow for one of their famed lobster suppers. Even though our tour bus had a washroom on board, we were never on the road for more than two hours at any given time. I watched the dozens of active seniors around me hold up their iPads at every scheduled stop, each happily waiting their turn to raise both arms up, to steady the tablet above their eyes like Moses, and capture the exact same photo as everybody else.

I had just wrapped up my first year in Toronto and was whisked away by my mother for a short holiday on the east coast. I had moved again for work, and it would be my third Canadian province in five years. It wasn't exactly marketed as such, but when I thought about it for a second, only retired people were interested in an all-inclusive sightseeing tour of Canada's Atlantic provinces. I slept for the bulk of the bus tour, especially through the tapes of Celtic folk songs the bus driver played, waking only intermittently to eat bland lobster rolls and greasy chips.

The group schedule had allotted ninety minutes to the Millbrook Cultural and Heritage Centre, an interpretation facility located on Mi'kmaq territory with a focus on history and artisanal crafts. The main tourist draw seemed to be the giant statue of Glooscap, who, we were quickly told by our tour guide, is a legendary figure in Mi'kmaq creation stories. As described through its didactic plaque, his name meant in Abenaki "a man from nothing," but a plaque alone was not enough to piece together a full story. After everyone had taken their snaps of the giant sculpture of Glooscap in the back garden, some milled about the glass vitrines and others concentrated on the offerings inside the gift shop. Chairs were quickly arranged in two half circles facing each other in the centre of the building, and everyone from the bus was ushered in to fill the seats. A young man coming off his break took centre stage, holding a hand drum across his arm. He closed his eyes and opened his mouth, and began to beat the drum skin in rhythm to a song sung in his language. The air always changes when drumming and singing begin, and I can't help but think this moment scares all the white people in the room. iPads and cameras slowly rose, and some of the older men shifted uncomfortably in their plastic seats. The young man finished his song and explained that this was a welcome song. He then introduced a young woman who came into the circle and started explaining the Millbrook centre's history: how Mi'kmaq people have lived there for thousands of years, and what can be seen on display in the multimedia vitrines and the artisanal gift shop. There was a question from the audience, from a guy on my tour bus. The staff handled it very politely. It was clear it wasn't the first time they had heard such a question—and, unfortunately, it probably would not be the last.

The middle-aged white man had raised his hand politely, like a Boy Scout, and self-affirmed that he grew up in Canada and was a Canadian. He had *spent his whole life in Manitoba*, he said, where *there were lots of Native people*, but he had *never heard of the Mi'kmaq before.* Somewhere between indignant and earnestly curious, he wanted to know, if Mi'kmaq people had existed for so long, then why hadn't *he* heard of them?

The man's tone had an accusatory ring to it—like, why didn't anyone from the Mi'kmaq Nation tell him about themselves? If he, being a Canadian man from Manitoba, had lived this long without hearing about Mi'kmaq people, then surely, maybe, they did not really exist.

His ignorant logic had an arrogance that no racialized person, new to this country or not, would ever hold. I was aware of the world of differences that existed between this man and myself, and between him and my mom, who also knew little to nothing about Mi'kmaq culture or the extreme degrees of violence enacted against Indigenous men, women, and children in the founding of Nova Scotia. But neither of us would ever assume our lack of information equalled anything beyond colonial narratives.

I only knew as much as any kid whose social studies

textbooks informed diligent readers via footnotes that "Micmacs" sided with the French. My mom knew only as much information as was included in the study notes for her citizenship test, which she took back in the early nineties and which upheld the story of Canada as being founded by loyal British subjects.

In reality, both my mother and I learned everything we knew about Canada's east coast history through watching Kevin Sullivan's 1985 made-for-television miniseries, *Anne of Green Gables*. We loved watching the series whenever it came on, which was at least twice a year and ran for three or six hours, depending on whether you also sat through the sequel where Anne leaves Avonlea and goes to Kingsport for a spell. We were not fans of the latter. It was the sheer force of Green Gables' kitschy allure that propelled me to even accept my mother's invitation to visit this end of the country in the first place. Lucy Maud Montgomery, the author of the beloved Avonlea books, has made it onto Canada's citizenship test as the correct answer to the only question mentioning Prince Edward Island. This is the information one learns on the way to becoming an official Canadian citizen. To date, no mention of Indigenous nations or treaties has ever made it onto an approved draft of the citizenship test. It's being worked on, though, allegedly, and the prospect that only new Canadians would have to know something about treaties and Indigenous histories is an idea I fully embrace, as that seems to be the best way for this country to shift.

What I would later learn on my own time was that, for hundreds of years, Mi'kmaq, Mohawk, Anishinaabe, Huron,

Seneca, and scores of self-governing Indigenous Nations traded amongst each other, and at times allied themselves with the rotating European traders of Holland, France, and Britain. They first helped the hapless Europeans survive the land, before helping them navigate trade routes and negotiate between themselves in times of both war and peace. Everything changed after the War of 1812, which, as a topic, is definitely on the citizenship test. The Dominion began to see Indigenous Nations as obstacles to settling the land, even after many Indigenous warriors assisted in holding off the Americans. The betrayal of those relationships, built over generations of covenants and wampum belts, is a disgrace all Canadians should know about. The failure of each successive Canadian government to uphold its end of treaty law is a shame all Canadians should bear.

Except we don't, because not enough people know the names, let alone the laws affecting Indigenous Nations across the regions.

Throughout our week out east, I sported a new canvas tote bag that read on one side "My Prime Minister Embarrasses Me" in a clean blue font on raw canvas. On the other side, it said the same in French. Designed by Pascal Paquette and Ellyn Walker during those last months of Harper in office, specifically targeting his negligence toward Indigenous rights and environmental issues, the words continue to ring true—no matter who's in charge. Harper was never popular in the Atlantic region, but I was still confronted with exasperating questions about the bag every day. Many people, on and off the bus, asked with curious smiles, *And where are you from?* They used a staccato rhythm that white people reserved pointedly for the feebled or racial-ized. *And where does your prime minister live?* they gently ask at each gift shop, parking lot, diner, and lighthouse. When I replied, *Ottawa*, the curious smilers are never embarrassed at themselves. They blink and keep smiling, sometimes chuckling, but still waiting for a response that affirms for them another reality, one where Canada is as pristine as its stolen glacier lakes, and where nothing bad has ever happened, at least to them. *I think we're doing pretty good,* said one woman who I didn't even slap in the face. *What were you expecting?*

In the city of Charlottetown, one shopkeeper guffawed at my bag and said that Stephen Harper was his favourite prime minister of all time. He was sitting as he said this, a mountain of a man on top of sandals and diabetic socks. He leaned forward with his arms on a cane. He had a tinge of an accent that was not quite British, not anymore. His wife, who had been hiding in a corner behind the cash register, scoffed at him and said that no one on this island agreed with him. I backed away and left them to grumble at each other inside of their empty Queen Street storefront. I wasn't here for any of this. I was just looking for a café where I could sit quietly and read until it was time to leave this town. I also wanted something to eat that hadn't been overboiled. It had been five days since I'd tasted a seasoning other than salt. The Atlantic provinces were real bonny and sweet, but everything that landed on the palate was oily and beige. Most of the people on the tour bus marvelled and squirmed when they were served fresh oysters for the first time in their lives. The same coos were offered at how delightful it was to eat mayonnaise with butter and lobster. As soon as we landed back in Toronto, my mom and I headed straight to what's left of the city's downtown Chinatown, a place neither of us have much history or connection with, except it's a place where we are never seen as tourists and where we can order a couple of stir-fried lobsters with ginger and scallions and taste home again.

The Island

Robbie was waiting for me, but he wasn't holding a sign or nothing. I just had to guess from the way he looked at me, watching without staring. I went out the main entrance of Gander Airport and saw a Busy Bee cab waiting, and knew that the old feller standing back in the lobby looking a little out of sorts was my guy. He was real nice and kinda sweet-looking in his oversized matching jacket and trousers, and asked me if I needed to stop for a bite to eat. He listed McDonald's and Timmy's, and it's not a bother to stop at either. They were next to all the major banks, too, as he gently reminded me that this fare would be cash only.

It had been a long travel day already for me, flying pre-dawn from Montreal to St. John's, waiting over three hours in a ninety-metre pen, before packing it in onto a fifteen-seater into Gander, a place most recently famous for its people's generosity. The city of Gander took in almost forty transatlantic flights en route to New York City on September 11, 2001. No other airport in the region would take them after four planes had already been forcibly diverted, but Gander kept its runways open and welcomed 7,000 strangers to a town of 10,000. I treated Robbie to a double-double after he said he wouldn't mind joining me for a cup. I ordered tea and a Caesar salad. It was all very Canadian, except Newfoundland is not very Canadian at all.

Once we were on the road, with the landscapes passing by, New-fund-lend was a real pretty place, we both concurred. Even though Robbie had already asked me, I told him again, yeah, I had been here before, but only on the east side of the province. I already knew from speaking to anyone from Newfoundland that no one outside of St. John's cared all that much about it. I really liked what I saw and heard, each time finding myself in a stranger's kitchen or shed, surrounded by a lot of laughter. Each visit confirmed that I had left Canada and its WASPy worries and empire hang-ups, and was settled in somewhere between Scotland and Saskatchewan, where everybody knew how to drink and every story was a lie built atop another lie, otherwise known as storytelling.

It was about an hour's drive from the airport to the ferry, but Robbie took it real nice and slow. *These here,* he said as we drove by a stretch of not-so-new housing developments, *these are what we call Alberta houses, after the province who pays for them.* An audible harrumph came at the end of his sentence. *But their economy is slowing down,* I replied, and he says, *Aye.* Always curious about regional cuisines, I asked Robbie what was good to eat around there—besides Timmy's—and he started speaking with renewed excitement about cod chowders and all sorts of sweets with caramel sauces and every type of berry, from wild blueberries to crowberries and partridge berries. He smacked his lips, as it was coming up on his suppertime, and he suggested that if I ended up missing the taste of Newfoundland, there was a store in Toronto where I could pick up a box of Jam Jams any day of the year. *There should be one in Alberta,* I offered back, and he agreed there should.

I didn't bother asking if there were any ethnic restaurants on the island, because there was always at least one Chinese restaurant everywhere, even on Fogo Island.

Robbie had been talking non-stop for forty-five minutes and I did not catch everything that was said. But my tongue started copying his intonations, the way it had when I was in Scotland for a stretch. First I stopped using the top of my jaw to speak, but rather slowed my consonants until they were just leaning against one another. Speakers of proper Queen's English would say I was slurring my words, but in fact, my enunciation was just starting to relax. Robbie had not made it up to Fogo in quite some time, but he'd heard from his wife's people, from Seldom on the south shore of the island, about how they built a big new inn on top of the old church in Joe Batt's Arm. This visual interpretation wasn't entirely off, but it did reveal how many Newfoundlanders have actually bothered to visit the now infamous inn.

After an hour and half, Robbie dropped me off at the ferry past the long line of cars waiting to board. We had eventually relaxed into a quiet zone that most people only share with loved ones and cab drivers, and a silent car ride can be pure pleasure. I was the only walk-on passenger and would have my pick of seats and views on the upper decks. As I tried to stretch out on a bench for a short nap, the clanging of vehicles coming on board and bodies climbing up to the passenger deck started to vibrate beneath me. My mind drifted to ferry-hopping across the Gulf Islands during the summer before I left Vancouver for good. For years, I had wanted to visit those islands, but never did until I knew I was finally leaving. That trip seemed like a lifetime ago, and yet, all those memories were alive again under my skin.

On the other side of the crossing, a younger feller named Andy picked me up in a big white SUV. All the staff of Shorefast were at a public lecture and screening by a British-Canadian artist, so a car from the inn was sent to fetch me. Andy was not as talkative as Robbie, but he had lots to say just the same. He was more self-conscious and talked about all the extra telephone poles and wires hanging all over the island, which were hardly noticeable to fresh eyes in comparison to the pristine blues and greens of land and sea. On the winding road up to the inn, Andy enthusiastically shared his admiration for how the architects really took care to cut into every different type of rock possible to show the glory of the island's contours. Suddenly more Scandinavian than Scottish, the outlines of the inn and each artist studio emerged from the mantel with a vibration that spoke to the past, present, and future in a single note.

Inside the inn's lobby and central hearth, dusk was dramatically setting through the building's floor-to-ceiling windows perched on the edge of the wild Atlantic Ocean. A roaring fire was well underway as the north wind started beating against the windowpanes. Instead of heading for the cinema to meet my hosts, I decided to explore the place from top to bottom. While locals colloquially refer it as the inn, the building is in fact a multimillion-dollar resort costing thousands of dollars per night. Helping myself to a complimentary cup of tea, I wandered from floor to floor, and when I reached the roof, I could not believe how no one was using these custom-designed outdoor hot tubs with ocean views. I would later be told quite adamantly that under no circumstances was I allowed to use any of the inn's amenities. Even as a joke to sneak back in for a soak, this proposition was not entertained for a second. The exclusivity of this building did not extend to the visiting artists, who may be invited in to perform, but were not to be confused with the actual clients of the inn.

Back on the second floor, I found a quiet corner where I could close my eyes and let the travel lag set into my limbs. I heard before I saw the man in a royal-blue cashmere sweater with designer eyewear talking on his phone. He was boasting to someone, presumably a business associate at the end of a longer work call, that they simply have to visit this place. *Yeah, it's a tiny island at the edge of the world called Fo-go. It's unbelievable... Yeah? ... I tell you, it's untouched.*

I refilled my cup of tea and sat on a custom-made cushion hand-embroidered with the words *Challenge for Change*, the name of the National Film Board's activist documentary film and video program that was in operation from 1967 to 1980. It was through Challenge for Change that I first heard and saw images of Fogo Island through my film professor's obsession with Colin Low and the twenty-seven documentaries he had made about Fogo and its people. For the longest time, I assumed Fogo Island was closer to Greenland than Canada, as the reels of black-and-white footage in my mind could not place this landscape or dialect as Canadian. Ethnographic from a class-based lens, Low's documentaries of a hardy but largely disenfranchised fishing community did not leave me with the impression that it was a place to visit—yet, here I was.

As fatigue set in, I started to wonder what I was doing here in the first place. I wondered if everyone who arrived on this island on the coattails of contemporary art shared in this thought. No sooner had my self-doubt kicked in than the first stragglers came out of the cinema where the artist talk had run long. There was immediately a reception behind me with bubbly and munchies. Out of habit, I tucked a few snack-sized bags of Cheezies into my tote bag for later. I struck up a conversation with a retired photographer who, along with his wife, split their time between Gander and Fogo when they were not travelling the world on artist residencies. As he continued to speak, I became deeply aware that I had just travelled for twelve hours within one leg of the country to arrive at this luxury destination. I wondered what Robbie would think about this reception, but realized in that moment why he had never been.

To my great surprise, I was generously given an entire saltbox home for my week-long stay, complete with three bedrooms and five beds. It's not one of the regular ones Shorefast uses, but they've rented another in Joe Batt's Arm for reasons not at first apparent. Each house is named after its owner, attaching each building to a homely but unknown presence. It's just a stone's throw from the inn, but in the darkness I am driven down and around curving roads I would trace by foot the following day. One jaunt around the winding hills on foot was enough for me to know that driving is the only way to get around the island. Iris, the residency coordinator, kindly dropped me off and got me settled in. I was offered one of the empty artist studios to work in if I liked, but I preferred to write within relative proximity to a working kitchen, and where I could get up in the middle of the night to add to an unfinished thought without having to hike through the darkness.

Before settling down each night to write at the kitchen table, I spent the better part of the day on my own, exploring different parts of the island. A few days in and not a single person had asked me where I was *really* from. I came from away, and that was enough. I began to realize my awe of Fogo wasn't just because of the landscape. Though the views *were* breathtaking. Every step in every direction was truly amazing. But what I really liked was how the water tasted sweet. How the air stung fresh and salty. I had also never before slept with my doors unlocked. The last time I attended an artist residency in a small, isolated place, my flat was broken into within the first week and all the electronics lifted, including the laptop I had hidden inside of my luggage. The local police said they could guess who did it, but there was no way to prove it unless he was caught doing it again. Here, on Fogo, I had to be repeatedly convinced that I didn't need to lock my car or front door. The gas station attendant noticed how I took the keys out of the ignition when I stepped out of the car and chuckled that he had to learn to do that when he'd lived in Halifax for a year. After years of parachuting into one place after another, consistently made aware that being different and from elsewhere could put me in harm's way, feeling safe on this island was a welcome change.

Obliged to follow artist-residency etiquette, even though technically I was just a visitor, I had a meet-and-greet with the three other visiting artists on the island. To no one's surprise, they were all from Cologne. I joined them for a couple more visits, but I was not up for networking. I got my social fill by stopping for chats here and there, from Joe Batt's Arm to south Joe Batt's Arm, to Tilting and back through Barr'd Islands and Shoal Bay, over to the town of Fogo and Fogo Central, and, of course, Deep Bay, too. I would have liked to visit Seldom, and Little Seldom, and Island Harbour, and maybe even the islands just off the island. Not since the Prairies had I enjoyed driving so much, whipping around the island in a cherry-red pickup truck listening to Selena Gomez on the radio. The ride came courtesy of my hosts. Everyone on the island knew that if you were in a red pickup, you were with Shorefast, and if you were in a white SUV, you were with the inn. Steffen spotted me in Deep Bay before we had even met and tried to follow me for a minute, but I just thought he was an aggressive tourist in his lemon-coloured Fiat. Steffen was a repeat visitor to Fogo and had become pals with Winston, and I really wanted to go fishing with Winston.

Winston Osmond's name had come up more than anyone else's on Fogo. A painter for about as long as—if not longer than—he was a fisherman, Winston knew what he liked to do. Before the inn had gone up, he had already started his own gallery and studio. When he was not fishing or gardening or making merchandise for his shop, he was painting local scenery from memory. I first met him on a search for postcards, and he seemed disappointed when I asked if he had painted any dogs. He knew what a fish looked like, so he painted those. He told me his ancestors had come as early as the 1700s from Britain, and how most people on Fogo were merchants from Newfoundland who had come up fishing and just stayed. *We all came from somewhere,* he said, looking past me. While there were lots of Osmond bones in the area, he too had left for Alberta and the Yukon, but had always come back. Most Newfoundlanders do. He knew the land and the sea and rocks tied him there. *When you leave and come back*, he said with arms wide open, *you head straight out to the ocean like greeting an old friend.*

There had been at least one reflective symposium on the island that asked whether international arts residencies needed to engage directly with the local community. From previous experiences, and the historical trajectory of colonization, I strongly believed in social engagement if these residencies were to happen at all. When I finally sat down with one of the directors of Shorefast, we spoke about the first couple of years of Fogo as well as my own research interests—namely, if the island had any ethnic people. After a brief pause that was not uncomfortable, at least not for me, I added, *Like, are there any legacies like businesses or restaurants run by non-European immigrants?* At this point, I had already been to nearly every shop and restaurant on the island, including the ice cream shop, the post office, the fancy restaurant, the regular restaurant, and the gas station that also served up fish and chips. I had spotted a Chinese-Canadian restaurant in the main town of Fogo, but it didn't look open for business. As we talked, I shared that my research interests widen into the region's Indigenous history with settlers, a history about which I knew nothing. Alex, who was also from away, acknowledged there were Beothuks, who were the original people on this land and were largely pushed out by European contact by the early 1800s. Google searches and history books would confirm all of this later, alongside the myth that Beothuks were an extinct people, but in sharing earlier drafts of this text, I would be corrected that many Beothuks fled south into Mi'kmaq communities, and that it was inaccurate and disrespectful to say otherwise. It's further complicated by the fact that many Mi'kmaq had to hide their own Indigenous ancestries through the cash bounty of the Scalping Proclamation put onto all Mi'kmaq men, women, and children by past governors Edward Cornwallis in 1749 and again by Charles Lawrence in 1756, neither of which have ever been officially repealed by the government.

Fogo was a summer fishing spot for some Beothuks, but as more English and Irish settlers arrived, their diseases and conflicts killed off scores of families living around the shores of Newfoundland, Labrador, and present-day Quebec. Alex told me about a plaque on the beach in Tilting, near the foot of Turpin's Trail, that framed Beothuks in a negative light. And while she had never seen the plaque herself, she suggested it might be worth going to if that was the kind of thing I was looking for.

The next day was grey and windy, and I took a ride along with Iris. The plaque looked more modern than I would have presumed. Under a sheet of stained Plexiglas, a text tells a settler-centric folklore of Michael Turpin, an Irishman who had settled in nearby Sandy Cove. He was allegedly attacked by Beothuks while potato farming with Patrick Murray, who survived to tell his tale. As we drove through Tilting, Ireland's flag could be seen over nearly every house, the green, white, and orange whipping proudly against the sea wind. The plaque's narrative suggested this attack on the two Irishmen was unprovoked, and carried with it a racist undertone painting Beothuks as inherently violent. The end of the plaque read:

The search party from Tilting found [Turpin's] body, but the Beothuks had gone. It is believed in the Spring of 1810, Turpin's head was found on a pole near high point on the exploits river. Apparently the Indians had used it for ritualistic or religious purposes as was their custom.

Nothing else is offered as to what happened before or

after this incident, except that the nearby hiking trail was named in Turpin's honour. I asked a few of the locals if they knew anything about the history of Beothuks who had lived on Fogo, and everyone I talked to seemed to know at least some Indigenous history. They knew that it was a tragic thing, what happened to the Beothuk people, but the issue is firmly resigned to the past. The summer fishing spots of Beothuks have long turned into ongoing fishing industries for generations of settlers, and any additional competition seemed unlikely.

Nowhere else in what is now Canada have I ever heard a fifth-generation middle-aged white man offer, unprompted, that his ancestors were immigrants—that they were all immigrants who came to this land. Most white settlers I have talked to in the rest of the country don't really know, let alone could they cite, Indigenous Nations by name on the lands they are inhabiting. No official narrative had led them to believe this land couldn't be owned and occupied, or that Aboriginal title was an ongoing economic right. The question over *Whose land?* was a misleading quagmire, as the notion of dispossession was a false framework that believed this land should ever be possessed at all.

By the end of the week, I heard another kind of story. As recently as the week prior to my visit, one of the international artists in residence had gotten the shit kicked out of him on the island. As the story went, he had gotten himself into a drunken brawl with some of the locals. Through second-hand information, I started to piece together that the visitor, a white German male in his late twenties, possibly thirties, had been heavily drinking, as he was reputed to do wherever he went as an international artist. Some teenagers were also drinking nearby, and something transpired between them, escalating into a physical fight. The mother of one of the teenage boys involved was livid, and, according to another kind of folklore, she had the artist banished from the island out of concern for the safety for her family. I heard the story from four different perspectives. The artist may or may not have been outnumbered and repeatedly kicked in the head, and he may or may not have provoked the fight with teenagers half his age and size. As soon as I had heard the story, through open gossip channels instead of from my hosts, I felt embarrassed and, unable to help it, I also felt all sense of safety vanish inside me. For once it wouldn't be my racial difference that made me stick out, but the nether class difference of being in the arts.

Amongst my peers, I have long observed that we circulated on cultural capital at the venture of cultural capitalists. Some artists truly believed holding cultural capital gave them real power, but their abuse of such limited resources revealed how weak they were outside of their bubbles. Here on this island, the inane qualities of artistic prestige had become the latest threat, both physical and psychological. The locals adapted their economies to feed themselves, but nobody wanted any trouble.

This kind of thing doesn't happen here. Until it does. And there will be no plaque to commemorate this occasion.

Difficult People

"The painters who would become involved with the Group [of Seven] were all children of British immigrants or immigrants themselves. Their nationalism was enfolded in the colonial project. They did not imagine an independent country, but pride of place within an Empire, a bastion of whiteness in a poly coloured world."
—Scott Watson, "Race, Wilderness, Territory, and the Origins of Modern Canadian Landscape Painting," in *Beyond Wilderness: The Group of Seven, Canadian Identity, and Contemporary Art*, ed. John O'Brian and Peter White, 2007

"This process does not require the actors in the system to question the status quo or how systematic constructions of race and culture affect their behavior and/or the institution's structure. Although many institutions of the dominant society claim to be objective or value free,

they actually reflect a specific cultural (that is, white) construction of reality."
—Patricia Monture-Angus, *Thunder in My Soul: A Mohawk Woman Speaks,* 1995

"While a strong argument can be made that non-European-descended peoples who come to live in Canada are also settlers, I am going to eschew the term here in favour of non-Black people of colour. This term will not be completely satisfactory either, because some non-European peoples are also able to access Whiteness, but it is a heck of a lot better than the term 'newcomers' which completely erases the history of communities that have existed in Canada for hundreds of years."
—Chelsea Vowel, *Indigenous Writes,* 2016

Two gymnastics hoops hang down from the rafters, gently swaying to the motion of the bodies around them. A single light shines down onto the floor, encircling several wooden bowls. I don't remember how many bowls there were, but I think there were three. *One bowl contains brown eggs. Another bowl contains a small mountain of red powder. One bowl remains empty.* No photographs were allowed for this performance, so I have to rely on my memory and the collective remembrance of Ursula Johnson's performance at VIVA! Art Action.

A rapt and silent audience of over one hundred bodies inched closer to the centre. Positioning themselves in various poses on the floor, the young sitting cross-legged, with one knee up or both legs tucked in on the cold cement floor. I stood a few rows in from the spotlight, behind other standing bodies, hovering over the heads of those sitting along the perimeter of the light. *The performer holds her space, entering slowly, unclothed, her hair loose around her bowed head.* I watched every gesture, every breath. *Kneeling down, sitting back onto the soles of her feet, the body readies itself for ritual and repetition. Taking a single egg, the performer hits it once, firmly, against the side of the bowl, cracking it and spilling its insides into the empty vessel.* Perhaps there were four bowls: one for the eggs' insides and one for their outsides. *This repeats over and over again, until the red powder is mixed in with the egg wash. The performer masticates the two ingredients together with her fingers, and slowly she begins smearing her limbs, her face, and most of her flesh with the bright ochre paint.* She reaches for and misses spots along her spine. *Her long hair is sometimes in the way, sometimes shielding. She is painting herself red. She stands up, grasping the handles, the body lurches back, not falling, but not standing up. The body remains in tension, pulling itself up, lurching forward, remaining in the same orbit.*

Red does not always resist. Red does not always mean stop. Red does not have to represent the blood that has spilled over 500 years of colonization. Red does not have to signify the skin colour those early settlers associated with all First Nations people, and is now unable to unsee and undo.

A few weeks later, I stepped into Ursula's installation work at the Art Museum. Unlike the Montreal audience, not everyone in Toronto looks like an artist. Everyone does, however, appear to be moving along the walls like an administrator. Inside the gallery, taking up almost an entire room, Ursula has built a moose fence into a one-way cage. Lots of people in patent leather shoes murmured *that this type of structure is how the Mi'kmaq traditionally hunt moose.* But along east-coast highways these wildlife fences are installed between the road and the bush to safely guide moose and deer along the side of the road. Viewers were permitted to enter the structure. The empty space reminded me of how enormous a moose can be. For others, the fence confronted them with their notions of colonial violence. For a few, the fence even reminded them of the holding pens at the Israel/Palestine borders. Even after hearing these other opinions, I still felt the size of a moose present in its absence. After a minute or so inside the cage, a baby-faced docent politely pointed toward the human-sized doors on either side so that we can exit and enjoy the rest of the exhibition.

Across the hall, a golden Jaguar sat parked on a photoshopped and printed vinyl Indian rug. The Jaguar had been twisted, as if giant hands had picked up the car and wrung it dry. *I am the American Dream (still just a Paki)/ Seminar Series on Race, Destruction and the many afterlives of a Paki: A private talk for one by your less than ideal Representative* first appeared in 2010 at Platform Gallery in Winnipeg. Acquiring a 1987 Jaguar Vanden Plas, considered by many the most decadent model of the luxury automotive brand, Divya Mehra went one step further by painting the car entirely gold before mounting her glorious trophy onto the wall as part of her first solo exhibition in her hometown.

The Jaguar brand holds an air of prestige for those who have lived in the British colonies. Driving, let alone owning, a Jaguar is a status symbol spilled over from the colonial empire and has remained a distinction of a rising middle class for the latter half of the twentieth century. In 2008, India's Tata Motors bought out the Jaguar Land Rover line from the Ford company, a long-standing champion of America's motor industry, who bought the line from British Leyland in the eighties. As a brand, JLR had been incurring loss for years, so when Tata paid US$2.3 billion for the line, the Ford company was grateful and publicly thanked the Indian company for doing them a favour. However, the first exchange between Tata and Ford was allegedly not so congenial. After a purported three-hour meeting in Detroit, Tata left feeling insulted by Ford, who wanted nothing to do with the megaconglomerate's then-new vehicle venture—and if they did, Ford felt *they* would be doing Tata a favour. Buying high from the British and selling low to India, Ford received sympathy from no one. Tata acquired JLR knowing this luxury brand would do well with India and China's rising middle class. Valued at over US$20 billion by 2017, JLR had hit upon a massive market that Britain—and America—were unable to see.

Seven years later, Divya's transformation of the Jaguar into a site of ruin remains difficult to see, but its rage was undeniable.

Almost up until the minute the artist panel begins, a small huddle of smokers and non-smokers try and form a game plan. The artists have all agreed to stomp their feet if any of them receives a bad question. Yaniya and I are supposed to be on guard, standing by if and when something racist happens.

Who is that guy? Yaniya asked once before, and again afterwards. I tried to describe the moderator: *He's white, he's pretty old, seems to work out a lot, loves the sound of his own voice. Typical.* Yaniya said that sounds nice, but both Divya and I vehemently shook our heads. *He's also known to be a creep,* I added, but even then, this description didn't remotely narrow down the field.

Yaniya grew up in Montreal and moved to Toronto around the same time I did. She was the first person to also wholly agree that Montreal is a fucking racist place. A few others have come forward since, and they are always Black people or people of colour. Most white and white-presenting people love Montreal too much to believe me when I say I really dislike being there. They think I am just being a contrarian. When they see that I am serious, they look wistfully away, saying, *Really? I love it there.*

It would make sense that this moderator was not on Yaniya's radar. She had to contend with too many white francophone men who love the sound of their own voice, but for someone who spent a lot of time on the Prairies, Robert's voice had been a mainstay, bolstered by his long-standing relationship with the only major English-language publication left outside of Ontario that spoke to the shadeless, amorphous mass that is Canadian art.

It didn't seem to matter that he did not connect with or understand the majority of the works or artists he was about to moderate. He was looked upon as a respectable and authoritative name in the Canadian art world. Just because for the first time the majority of artists representing "Canada" were non-white, and almost all women, why should structures like artist panels or after-parties be organized any differently? After all, award ceremonies are rarely for the recipients.

Coming into the lecture hall, the young white student volunteer at the door let everyone through, but stopped Divya to double-check her name. Once everyone was seated onstage, Robert started things off with a quote from Northrop Frye. He set the tone at postwar Canadiana, and that is where the panel conversation stayed. The event was over before it had a chance to begin, ending over sixty years in the past at the height of postwar literary criticism and with outdated inklings of what the national imagination of Canadian art and identity could be. He had words to say about each of the artists on the panel but really only spoke at length about a couple of the works—works that just so happened to be by the two white artists. Bridget and Jacynthe were unable to deflect and bring in their fellow panelists. They didn't know they should have been answering questions about reconciliation as white settlers and to talk about their cultural heritage and privilege instead of speaking only about their art practice. No one ever asked them, so how could they know.

After being unable to keep up with Raymond, laughing at Divya, and avoiding Ursula, the moderator opened up the discussion to the floor. The first question came from a man in the balcony. His voice, trembling, was shrill with anger. I imagined him shaking, growing pink in the face above his neckline, his bow tie sitting askew. He went into a tirade about how he found a single work by an unspecified artist to be personally offensive to someone like him. Being a true WASP, he did not name names, but he needed everyone present to know that he was made to feel incredibly uncomfortable. He was so angry that an artwork had the audacity to be so aggressive to its viewers, who, he must have believed, were all just like him.

Without seeing his face, I thought he sounded a lot like the man who got into Divya's face at her opening earlier in the fall. He had charged up to her, introduced himself, and then scolded her by shouting that she was being completely incomprehensible to him and that she was being such a difficult person.

Another question was fielded from another white man, sitting a few rows in front of me. His question was for Ursula, but it was also really more of a comment. He thanked her for her work and said the piece reminded him about the impact of residential schools. He appeared moved by his own empathy.

Robert looked like he desperately wanted to wrap the panel up. He barely even looked out for questions. I don't think he intentionally ignored my hand sticking up from the back of the room so much as he didn't have it in him to look out that far. The question I wanted to ask, but never got to, was about legibility. The question that burned inside of me was whether anyone up there even considered themselves legible in terms of Canadian art and identity. So far, the default for both had been whiteness, or settlers of British/European heritage, but as the majority of the artists, for the first time, were neither, did they feel there were layers of missing knowledge between them and the dominant culture, who know little to nothing about Other histories, cultures, and experiences? With this invisible barrier in place, I wanted to know if their work felt visible here, in this context, and what were their strategies and coping mechanisms?

Hours later, I posted the question online and grew angrier as people "liked" it without ever having to answer it.

The panel and exhibition were all ancillary to the only major award for mid-career artists in a country with a wide berth and a low ceiling. Regionalism is trotted out like some backwater competition that leads to the national finals. Divided into five general regions, the country we call Canada is reduced to a shortlist of artists under the age of forty, accompanied by jury members representing each region who are usually over the age of forty. The whole affair was chaired by a representative from the National Gallery of Canada, and in 2017, an international juror was added into the mix—and of course, "international" meant "European." While the shortlist supposedly reflected the "diversity" Canadians so crave, the assembled seven-person jury was frighteningly white-presenting—frightening for them, as they would have to collectively wring their hands over who would be the least offensive but most politically correct artist to award this prestigious and seemingly innocuous prize to.

Two hours before the gala where the winner would be announced, the *Toronto Star* had already leaked the winner's name. I was told it wasn't the first time they had done this, and I doubted it would be the last. It is already violent to pit artists against each other for elite enjoyment, let alone be turned into a media scoop. No matter how much of a dog-and-pony show it became, artists have cared, and still care, as even being nominated is seemingly the only tangible validation in a country that expects you to make it elsewhere. Still, every year, we are reminded how important the award has become because look at who has already won. Brian Jungen won the first one in 2002. Annie Pootoogook in 2006. In 2008, Tim Lee took home the prize—only one of two times in the award's history that a person of colour had won at that point. Ursula's win would be the first time the Atlantic region had ever won. For the 150th year of Canada's confederation, for 150-plus years of ongoing colonial violence, a strong contender from the east coast, one of two Indigenous artists shortlisted for the first time ever, Ursula was going to win. Her strong artistic practice made the decision easier. Everyone should feel good about this. But not everyone does.

I spent the majority of the evening hanging out with Americans in town for the Toronto Art Fair. I felt drawn to them, because they had nothing to lose or gain from the evening's proceedings. The Americans didn't know or care about Canada's regional politics. They were mostly confused by how a country this size can be boiled down to five artists, especially when the shortlisted artists were all operating on completely different levels and at varying points in their careers. The exhibition itself told them nothing about the pulse of Canada, which in and of itself speaks volumes about how we see ourselves.

At the after-party, large white men in suits were standing everywhere, their meaty paws clutching tumblers of melted ice. No one knew where they had come from. The majority of artists of colour were now pressed against the wall, unwilling to dance to Hall and Oates. Raymond was determined to cut up the dance floor. Bridget looked so happy that it was all over. Ursula had the biggest smile in the room. The atmosphere was thick with desire and disappointment. Images of artist-decorated rooms flashed across flat-screen TVs hanging above the bar. Thirsty established curators prowled around the bar, buying anyone they could a drink. Social climbers lunged across tables to grasp arms, to say *Hey* to important people passing through this party and town. Heterosexual couples dry-humped in brightly lit corridors, and the sloppy salutations of those entering and exiting the party left sticky traces on each other's cheeks. Any semblance of art as separate from capitalist corporate culture had vanished a long time ago.

For most of the evening, I sat in a corner next to Cara, an artist from Virginia. We chatted as if we were on a road trip driving through one terrible party after another. Near the end of the night, Cara turned to me and said flatly that it felt like we were at a Kinko's office Christmas party, but way worse, because these people *believe*.

Yes, I sighed, scanning the room one more time, *except I would rather be at a corporate office party, because at least it would feel more honest.*

375

It's early on Sunday when I wake to a knocking outside the room. Billie is still asleep as I roll out of bed to answer the door. I find some clothes on the floor to put on, and she blindly reaches out for me, trying to pull me back into bed.

Bleary-eyed and suddenly alone in bed, Billie checks the time on her phone and sees that it's not even 8:00 a.m. She can't tell if the knocking is coming from outside the bedroom door or outside the apartment. There are two girls staying in the spare bedroom—a blonde and a brunette—but what would they want at this hour? No, the knocking is coming from farther away. A door opens somewhere to the outside world. Awake but still groggy, Billie hears me talking to someone: a man speaking English with a thick Québécois accent. His voice is agitated. He has been knocking on every apartment door in the building, searching for his grandfather's watch.

When I open the door and see this guy in his mid to late twenties standing there, my first instinct is that he is looking for drugs. His eyes look desperate, but he appears remorseful for waking me up. He tells me he is searching for two American girls he met the night before at Osheaga who went back to his place for a party. By "party" he means he hooked up with one while the other passed out drunk. His grandfather's watch was last seen on his bedside table and is the only thing he has left of the man who raised him. He has searched his house high and low all morning, and backtracked his Uber-ride history to this apartment building across town. Those two girls are now asleep in Billie's spare bedroom, which is being actively rented out during those work-free, care-free Montreal summers.

I let Billie take over, as this was not my home. She tries defusing the situation by relating to him calmly that she, too, was raised by a grandparent. When he learns that those two girls are staying in the spare room, he refuses to leave until he has talked to them. The stench of his body spray would linger for days in the front hallway. The girls are hysterical and do not help the situation. Billie tries to convince him that calling the police is not going to solve anything. After a futile search and a lot of yelling and crying, he leaves empty-handed.

Within an hour, two police officers show up at the door. Billie hates talking to the cops, but they ask to speak with the tenant of the apartment. She thinks those two girls probably took it, either as a joke or just to be cruel in the way young women can be. She doesn't say this to the cops. She just wants everyone out of her space. The blonde and the brunette easily sweet-talk the cops away before they rush back for Sunday dinner in Connecticut, and promise Billie they'll write an excellent Airbnb review, which will never materialize.

It is just another day, another drama, of life in Montreal.

Neither of us had ever been to Osheaga, an annual music festival that brings in over 100,000 people, many of them young and wasted, to listen to hundreds of live bands and DJs on Île Sainte-Hélène off the Hochelaga Archipelago on the St. Lawrence River. The summer season in Montreal was a great income period for the perpetually underemployed who had a spare room or an entire apartment to let to the hordes of incoming visitors for festivals, Grand Prix, and other international events. Branding would be everything.

Osheaga officially acknowledged that it is named after Hochelaga, but that was about the extent of the connection. Like most culturally appropriated words used to designate streets and cities and the country itself, the original etymology of *Hochelaga* has sparked minor interest, with different interpretations coming from different people. Everything from *beaver dam* to the *Lachine rapids* to a bad translation of *Oshahaka*, which in Kanien'kehá:ka is translated as *the people of the hand*—possibly a teasing reference to the European custom of insistently shaking hands. Hochelaga was also considered to be a large, thriving village of the Haudenosaunee Confederacy along the St. Lawrence, in today's measurements roughly the distance between the river and Rue Sherbrooke, and spanning Pie-IX and Préfontaine on the metro's green line. Jacques Cartier detailed Hochelaga upon his first visit but was unable to find the village on his second trip. No settler has found it since. With speculation that traces of the village must be beneath the city streets, possibly closer to or on top of Mont Royal, the city of Montreal and the provincial government launched a series of test digs between Rue Outremont toward Rue McGill in 2017, coinciding with Montreal's 375th anniversary, 482 years after Cartier's initial records for the first official search for Hochelaga.

It was this summer when Billie and I decided to live together for a month in Montreal. It would be the beginning of the end of our long-distance relationship. We had been together for about a year, travelling between Toronto and Montreal at least once a month to see each other. Even though we hated visiting each other's cities, we managed to make it work for a while.

I really didn't understand how people could live in Montreal for more than a year, and she thought the same about Toronto. In Montreal, nothing ever changes and nobody ever works. Walking down the same side streets of Jeanne-Mance and Durocher, I paid no mind to the hipsters or the Hasidic Jews, who have never paid mind to me. Being invisible comes with both frustrations and advantages. Walking around any up-and-coming neighbourhood, I am aware that someone like myself usually presents a signal towards increasing property prices. I have heard time and again that my people, the Chinese, are like rats: where there's one, there will be more moving in.

When Billie moved north of Jean-Talon, I went grocery shopping for the both of us. People at least talked to me here, not like in Outremont. The Greek men were especially keen to start a conversation, and they kept asking me where I *really* came from. I can see them eyeing me from over their newspapers and coffees with a fixed stare, calculating in their mind my wide forehead, the shape of my eyes, my broad nose, the pallor of my skin—assuming that I am likely from Korea, Japan, or China. The vast cultural differences between these countries is of no importance to their line of unsolicited questioning, and they won't take Toronto for an answer either. I am aware that the Greek woman behind the cash register never smiles at me, even though I come in a lot. I can't help but notice how she smiled at Billie the first time I brought her to the store. No one can ever guess Billie's cultural heritage, and those who try are often men who do so as a way of flirting. Maybe in the distant future, her mixed Eastern European and Arab roots will be more legible, but for now, her dark, wavy mane and light-skinned face can still pass for Mediterranean to most Greeks. Most Arab women can clock her from down the street, and Billie, in turn, has been learning to see them, too.

I am the first non-white person she had seriously dated, and, combined with her own mixed-race awakening, Billie started to feel through her allyship, maintaining the privilege of whiteness but also beginning to see and feel the pressures of racial oppressions growing inside her. As it goes, she began to hold the pain and trauma of a racialized person alongside the power of white fragility. In her efforts to educate herself, she started attending a group of anti-racism meetings led by white people. She invited me to come to one, and, to everyone's surprise, I went, because love clouded my better judgment.

We take the 80 Parc bus to the meeting being organized by a middle-aged white woman named Ann. She begins the evening by admitting it's hard to be honest in a colonized space. She continues to admit her ongoing grief and connection to the violence of white supremacy in this country we call Canada. Ann owns her whiteness and all of its tribulations with every word she speaks. Billie admires Ann and marvels at her speech. I think this Ann woman is just being a decent person, but I go along with it because this seems important to Billie. Even though racialized people have been saying the same things for decades, it will always be heard more resoundingly when a white person says exactly the same thing.

By the time the meeting begins, about twenty people have convened in the room, representing a range of age, race, and gender. Jacob is also there at this meeting. He is a figure who haunts every art event in town, and it's always nice to see him bopping around from one gathering to the next. He has lived in Montreal for over twenty years and doesn't speak any French, but, being an anomaly, he's a straight white Anglo man who is well-liked by everybody.

To my initial disappointment, I mainly see predominantly white cis women gathered in the room, but Billie is quick to correct me to not presume other people's genders. There are at least half a dozen racialized people here, predominantly Black-presenting, so I at first don't think anything strange is going on. I'm not the only racialized person here. That's usually a good sign, but I have momentarily forgotten I am in Montreal. A year into visiting the city and its scenes on a frequent basis, I have still never gotten used to the social dynamics in this town, where everyone is so chill, until suddenly they are not. There is so much hidden drama being pulled in from all directions at any given time. In a place with almost no professionalism, everything feels deeply personal and, therefore, political.

Everybody in the room helps to rearrange the communal furniture into a U shape around a pop-up screen. The meeting's format gives space to a screening and discussion as we sit through the seventeen minutes of René Vautier's *Afrique 5o*.

The first purportedly anti-colonial film from France isn't remotely decolonial, despite a disclaimer given at the beginning of the meeting that decolonization, in the framework of Eve Tuck and K. Wayne Yang, is not meant to be employed as a metaphor and is most apt when used in connection to the land rights of Indigenous Nations. As the video finishes, I wonder if I should just leave right then and there. With zero surprise and some anguish, I see that decolonization is still very much being used as a metaphor. The pomposity and energy of postwar white French Marxists realizing the extent of their country's colonial atrocities was, and remains, fifty years later, navel-gazing, at best. The camera can't help but objectify and speak for the Black bodies in its gaze. There is only entitlement and romance of the filmmaker's own conscious awakening. I wonder if the filmmaker has made this work to show how monstrous his fellow countrymen have been or if he really made it to prove to himself (and himself alone) that he is not one of those monsters.

Throughout 2017, it felt like this was the year white people were waking up to the racial oppressions happening all around them, but I am still not sure if they will do anything helpful about it. There's never been a shortage of middle-class white boys and girls with poverty politics espousing politically correct rhetoric, but their humble self-reflection remained in short supply.

The guest facilitator for the evening is Antony, a white-presenting cis man in his late twenties, maybe early thirties, with a European accent. He has learned to never speak first. After Ann introduces him, he conjures the recent scandal of the Saint-Jean-Baptiste Day parade, also known as Quebec's national holiday, where somehow a float of all white people end up being pushed by a volunteer crew of young Black students. Antony doesn't form a strong opinion about it either way, but calls our attention to the news event as a local starting point in relation to screening *Afrique 50*. He says all of this in French. I pick up bits and pieces, but mostly rely on a whisper translation from Billie. I have already heard about the Jean-Baptiste incident, which recalled for many an insensitive image of slavery, and for others who don't see race, it was all merely an unfortunate coincidence.

At one point during the heated discussion that follows the screening, two Black-presenting individuals discuss the outright hostility they feel in Montreal, the city they were each born into and subsequently pushed out of through relentless systematic discrimination. It doesn't matter if they grew up here and speak only French, but being Black, they feel they would never belong to the essentialized Québécois identity. Then another Black-presenting person speaks up and says she has never felt disenfranchised because of her biracial background. She tells the room in English that she doesn't identify as Black and doesn't identify as white. In the same breath, she catches herself and also tells the room of the stinging microaggressions she's experienced from the people closest to her.

I don't know what to do with any of this information. It stays inside of me for a long time. Billie isn't sure if I should include this part in the story, but also doesn't want it to be cut. Billie reaches out to Ann and Antony and mentions that I feel really fucked up from attending their meeting and am probably going to write about it. They both say they look forward to reading about it. When Billie relays this message back to me, I feel mad, like, fuck, now I have to write this story for these white people to read so that they can better understand why their race meeting failed?

The conversation that night, every night, inevitably returns to the only issue any of us has ever consistently heard in Quebec: the history and disenfranchisement of the French. Discussions of racial oppression feel at least a full decade behind in this province, and at least one person has been quick to defend that the delay is the lag time it takes to translate contemporary race theory into French. At the first mention of the Great Darkness, I squeeze Billie's hand, indicating that I want to go. She gives a firm squeeze back, but I already know she is going to stay until every chair has been folded and put away. Public conversations on anti-racism in Montreal never get beyond introductory 101 levels. The conversation always stalls on French oppression. You can't move it, no matter what happens, and its dominance is explained to outsiders through a patronizing, dismissive wave, because how can an outsider ever fully understand? As the conversation goes around in circles, Jacob manages to land a good point: the Québécois have never been colonized. They were dominated, they have been oppressed, but they have never been colonized. This distinction is important, and from the looks on some faces in that room, this distinction has yet to be processed.

In Quebec, anyone from a non-anglophone or non-francophone heritage technically counts as diverse. As leftover policy from the mindset of Pearson's "two founding nations" rhetoric, diversity in Quebec has also overextended its use of the word *Métis*, which does not refer to the Métis of the Red River Settlement or the Métis Nation of Alberta, but quite plainly translates as *mixed*. A lot of people are getting confused, though, or downright greedy about being mixed, and they are starting to vigorously claim Indigenous heritage as their ancestral right. I look this up after hearing how a disproportionate number of new Métis are coming out of Quebec, with census numbers confirming that those self-identifying as Métis have risen by over 50 per cent in the ten-year span from 2006 to 2016. Some of the new Métis, or nouveau Métis, are forming clans and reconnecting to their "heritage" by trying to scheme what they believe is theirs, including ill-informed ideas about tax evasions and extended health coverage. In clan meetings, it's been reported by the *National Post* that the new members trade knowledge about which stores are willing to accept their self-made Métis membership cards; whether there are tax loopholes for big purchases if they get items delivered to reserves where they have never lived; and how to access free health care for overdue dental work. Determining someone else's Indigeneity as a non-Indigenous person is not a stop on my search. I only skim the essays by Indigenous scholars and activists who consistently refute any legitimacy in "self-indigenization." The issue isn't whether they may or may not have Indigenous blood somewhere in their ancestry, but that blood quantum alone does not qualify for nationhood. That logic works only in settler culture, where if a person is any percentage of any race other than the dominant one, then that person's perceptibly weaker bloodlines can be used to represent their cultural values with both authentic and oppressive authority. What interests me is how in Canada, white settler culture refutes any colourful persons claiming Canadian culture as their own, but will be the first to claim their one-sixteenth blood as justification enough to own that history and knowledge in its full entitlement. Even if a person lives their entire life with all the benefits of whiteness, many are shamelessly taking up space meant for those with fewer advantages.

Billie looks white, but she isn't the right kind of white. She was brought up in the first-generation Eastern European sense of whiteness, with most of the advantages of being white-presenting but the oppression and discrimination of not being a WASP. For the arts organizations that invite her to work with them, her presence allows them to check their diversity box. It's why she kept quiet for so long about being not quite white. Coming out as half-Arab also meant handing over a big self-congratulatory pat on the back for the white arts organizations that work with her. She gets to be the "diverse" person in the group, but the one whose suggestions to actually diversify go unsupported. As the only remotely racialized person on her board, Billie made the suggestion to her fellow colleagues to consider doing land acknowledgements during the 2017–18 programming year. She tried to frame how the gesture would call attention to the fact that Montreal sits on Kanien'kehá:ka land and that their artist-run centre was aware of the significance of 375 years of occupation.

But it's no longer their land, one of her peers responded.

I don't think this is appropriate for art events, another offered.

Non, was the clearest answer.

Through over a year of meetings, Billie repeatedly offered up different ways to decentre whiteness on a board that brought her on to do exactly that, but she was repeatedly outnumbered. A few of the other white-dominant artist-run centres have featured full-year programming of Indigenous artists and have continued to congratulate themselves about it. Nobody seems to remember an Indigenous-led exhibition by Kanien'kehá:ka of Kahnawake curator Ryan Rice called *Hochelaga Revisited* from less than ten years prior, and the integrity that could come with hiring Indigenous curators on an ongoing and permanent basis rather than as honorary guests.

When Billie tells me of another board meeting that kept up with status quo, I ask her why she keeps giving so much energy and time to this racist organization. She doesn't defend them but explains her devotion out of her sense of commitment to her community, because she feels obligated to at least try. She also likes everybody on her board, and they like her when they run into each other at openings and performances. In closed-door meetings, though, no one is willing to take her suggestions with an ounce of seriousness. To do so, they would have to get uncomfortable. And if she has learned anything about her white peers, especially when they think they are among only other white people, it's that they get really upset and defensive when they are made to feel remotely challenged about their whiteness. This was her community, and it has always been clear that it would never be mine.

During that summer in Parc Ex, Billie would run into a woman named Andrea who first left her feeling shook up. In her first encounter with Andrea, Billie sees her standing on a corner across from St. Roch Park. They catch each other's eye, as strangers do, on a neighbourhood sidewalk. After learning she is Cree, Billie tells her she has just been hanging out with some folks from Whapmagoostui, and upon hearing the familiar word, Andrea immediately cries. When she feels more comfortable with Billie, Andrea begins a conversation about not having enough money, and asks if Billie has any to share. It is the only time Billie has opened her wallet and handed over a bill to someone she barely knows. Andrea talks with her new neighbour about how much she misses her family up north. Billie listens with full attention. She knows how expensive it is to travel in either direction, and how isolating that kind of distance can be within a province that thinks the north ends at Rimouski. When they part ways the first time, Andrea surprises Billie with a big hug. She looks happy to be held firmly and squeezed back.

In Montreal, being Cree is often assumed as James Bay Cree, who, as a Nation alongside Naskapi Innu across Northern Quebec, agreed in 1975 to a celebrated and controversial treaty. Lauded as the first modern-day treaty for land-rights negotiations and economic development, the James Bay and Northern Quebec Agreement gave up vast amounts of land in exchange for cash compensation and the right to self-govern. One of the many boards and corporations formed from this agreement was the Cree school board, which commissioned the formation of a non-profit arts organization to bring Indigenous and non-Indigenous artists into remotely located Cree schools. Billie is periodically employed by this organization, which is headed by white people and employs predominantly white people. They try to hold their white privilege while working with Indigenous communities facing high rates of youth suicide and depression, but I have doubt in my heart about this logic that still translates into employment for settlers. Everyone who works there must go through a training process involving workshops with Cree representatives as well as participating in the blanket exercise. While the mandate of the organization is to prioritize Indigenous artists and teachers, there always seem to be a shortage of finding Indigenous artists available, and non-Indigenous people end up filling those roles instead.

It'd been a while since Billie had steady work, so I held off for months until the winter season before gently asking her what she honestly thought about non-Indigenous people running this organization and bringing non-Indigenous artists into these communities. Neither of us wanted to have this conversation, as increasingly our discussions on race had not gone well. There had been more and more instances where she had been privy to racist things said by white people who believed they were amongst only white people, or conversely where she was called out for being racist by racialized people because of her access to whiteness. Within the confines of our intimacy and my understanding, she could share how upset she was, even when she heard anti-Asian sentiments from some of her oldest friends, all of whom were wealthy WASPs. Some of them knew she was dating an Asian person, that we had just visited Hong Kong together to visit my family, but they said what they said, and in the end, Billie did nothing except come home to tell me about it. Somehow in these moments, she had become the person who was seeking validation and comfort, except I never gave her any. After each blowout, when I would eventually ask her through my hurt why she did nothing, her responses were always the same abdication: she either couldn't risk losing these people in her life or couldn't wait to get them out of her life.

When I happened to meet one of her colleagues from the Cree arts organization at another wealthy person's New Year's Eve party, I was startled by just how white her colleague, and the party, was. We were party crashers, catching a ride out of the city with her friends for a random adventure that led us to a private ski chalet just north of Toronto. From the moment we pulled up, our carload had stuck out sorely with our lack of Christmas sweaters and cottage provisions. As the night wore on and everyone headed out for their annual cross-country ski in the moonlight, Billie and I stayed behind. Neither of us had ever learned to cross-country ski. Instead, we got ready for bed and my thoughts tumbled out. I asked her if it wouldn't be better for these youth up north to see reflections of themselves instead. I could feel before I could see the walls go up behind her eyes. Her body shifted away from mine and she slowly responded that it was dangerous of me to say what is and isn't better for self-determined communities. When her voice, her entire body, broke, she couldn't believe I was judging her when she had already told me why non-Indigenous people worked there. Through tears of frustration, she told me how these kids were killing themselves and how this program tried to help them.

We were lying next to each other all this time, but we were so far apart.

Epilogue

It was May 27, 2018.

My family arrived in Edmonton, Canada, exactly thirty years ago this day.

I didn't know what to do with myself, so I just did what I usually do on a Sunday. I woke up slowly, at first sunlight, in my bed in the apartment that I rent in the west end of Toronto. I read. I stretched. I drank a green smoothie as I watered my indoor plants. Even though I mostly have succulents, they are barely alive, being damaged by my frequent absences and the rotation of subletters who over/undercare for them. I don't like grocery shopping on weekends, so I looked in the fridge and made myself a skillet breakfast of scraps: leftover fiddleheads, one hot-house tomato, one large free-run egg, and one Toulouse sausage. A simple fry-up. When it's plated and I sit down to eat, I take a photo first and send it to my mother, who lives in Vancouver. The only words I write in this message are *30 years*. No sentiments of happiness preface this statement. Just a record of time passed.

What does it mean to have lived in Canada for thirty years? For starters, it means I have a lot of privilege. I recognize and affirm how my life would have been really different if my mother had stayed in Kowloon. I actually can't imagine what I would be doing now in that case, but I know it wouldn't include this opportunity to write a publicly funded book about my life as an art critic. I also recognize that this privilege of citizenship comes at a cost, and the expense of my personal advantages has been unequally redistributed against anyone who doesn't fit neatly into this ongoing colonial project.

I send the photo of my homemade breakfast to my mother because she likes to know what I'm eating and that I'm still finding time to cook for myself. I wish we could share a meal together on this day. It's been thirty years of an easier life with more personal freedoms, and it's been thirty years of feeling estranged, with constant reminders of how we don't belong. I can't say it's a particularly joyful feeling, but it's an event I would have marked with a meal. This is how we celebrate, and how we mourn—by eating together or cooking for each other. In Vancouver or Toronto, or even if we had found ourselves back in Edmonton, we would have likely gone for dim sum. While dim sum is a Cantonese tradition, and my mother was raised in the northern cities of Beijing and Tianjin, she was first dislocated to Kowloon in 1974 for fourteen years, where early-morning dim sum became the norm. She had actually forgotten that it had been thirty years since we moved to Canada. This year, she only remembered it has been forty-four years since she arrived in Kowloon. She only remembered her first dislocation date, but moving forward, I will try to remember both for her.

My mother left mainland China for Kowloon when the latter was still under British rule. She wanted to get away from Mao's then-ongoing reign that saw millions of people starved, tortured, and beaten to death, only for millions more to turn on each other through a mass hysteria of discipline and punishment. Even though Mao died in 1976, my mother did not trust history would not repeat itself. When the handover of Hong Kong loomed, she knew she had to leave, again.

I never learned any official histories of China beyond what I have read in fictional novels and newspaper articles addressing anniversaries of "the Great Leap," "the Great Famine," and the countless conflicting Western interpretations of "the Cultural Revolution." I only partially understood how the British invaded Shanghai in the north and Canton in the south, importing massive amounts of opium that destabilized the country so they could set up shop. The Republic of China lasted for only thirty-seven years on the mainland, until the Nationalists fled to Taiwan from the Communist uprising. Over the last decade, I learned my maternal great-grandfather was Sun Baoqi, a foreign minister and premier in the Republic of China. Everything he built would eventually be dismantled. These are just the tips of threads I have barely begun to unravel.

Only lately have I started asking the right questions of my mother for her to start telling me her own history. I take down notes, but I don't have a full grasp of the stories being relayed, being twice removed from understanding a history of a place I have never lived, yet feeling so close to the paratext through the familiar timbre of my mother's voice. We speak to each other in different languages, asking and answering only in Mandarin and English, or a version of Mandarin and a version of English that only she and I can understand and that no other Mandarin or English speaker would be able to decipher. This is where her history and mine lives, in this compromise of language.

PART II

By the time I left Edmonton, there were a number of growing neighbourhoods where you could hear at least a dozen different languages being spoken in grocery stores and shopping malls. Since the early 2000s, immigration into Canada by visible minorities had steadily spread across the country, with a larger percentage of settlement occurring in the Prairies instead of in the three urban centres for the first time in history.

Up until a couple of years ago, I had never learned or sought out the backstory of how Britain came into possession of Rupert's Land. I am still not entirely sure how the Hudson Bay Company legally owned the land in the first place to sell. I am only starting to read about the Crown's use of treaties to begrudgingly share the land with Indigenous Nations, if you can call .05 per cent of the original land mass "sharing." I never knew that contact and trade occurred for hundreds of years before the Crown turned against their hosts, who had helped them to survive the climate as well as fend off the Americans. The only thing I do know is that from pre-Confederation to present day, only white and white-presenting people are still unequivocally considered citizens under colonial law. There is a great lack of human rights in this country for Black people who are profiled, harmed, and incarcerated at grossly disproportionate rates; for migrant workers and refugees ignored and abused by the brutalities of state politics and bureaucracies; and for Indigenous communities who do not have the basic necessities of clean drinking water and adequate shelter. This general apathy towards each other, specifically the Other that is not white, remains an everyday reality in Canadian civility. As a nation-state that is increasingly multicultural in the self-guiding sense of the word rather than the state-controlled/nation-building-project sense, whiteness still remains the default for normality, for respectability, if not acceptability, under ongoing colonial laws.

Growing up under the myth of multiculturalism, I was under the impression that all of my non-white classmates and I were only variations of each other, and that, most importantly, we were to be understood as minorities to the white majority. I always presumed that I was a guest, a foreigner just visiting this host country, and I might eventually have to return to a home that was no longer mine. For the first three years in Edmonton, we ended up moving around every year. After each move, I had stubbornly refused to take off my coat whenever I went to school or to visit a friend's house. This went on for months. My mother thought I was adapting to the dry, frigid climate of our new surroundings, but I just never felt like I was going to stay long enough anywhere.

Over the span of thirty years, I have learned to never feel Canadian in identity, being cognizant that this label has historically described only a polite white person who is not American. This facade of politeness could be interpreted as a hangover from British mannerisms, a false benevolence made only in comparison to America. Or, in the wake of an impossible and imaginary nationhood, politeness was just another lie that was repeated until it felt true. Canadian identity formed on the implicit bias that believed northern European whites like the English and French were racially superior and the sturdiest stock to survive the "Great White North," an exclusion that conveniently erased all Indigenous people and would form the backbone of decades of exclusionary immigration policy that could turn away immigrants of African and Asian descent based on the grounds of "climatic unsuitability." Politeness, in other words, was a passive-aggressive concealment of deeply racist attitudes and the seemingly non-threatening systems that held these beliefs firmly in place.

While I don't necessarily feel Canadian, I also don't feel wholly Chinese anymore either. After thirty years away, I now feel the least Chinese when I am in China. I have been tainted with Westernized foods, fashion, and ideas. I have only grown to appreciate my visits to Hong Kong after a long period of frustration. I almost feel like I could belong if I never opened my mouth to speak. I think this appreciation has come from accepting that while I come from this place, I will likely never be able to live there again. When pressed about where I come from, I will say I come from Alberta. I come from Edmonton. Citing the non-descript Canadian city I grew up in, it's often heard more as a joke, especially in Toronto, when I relate more to their idea of a tar-sand pit full of rednecks driving pickup trucks than I do to a WASP mentality. I spent over twenty years there, from 1988 to 2010, the longest stretch I have spent in any one place. They were my formative years. I learned to see the world within the boundaries of Treaty 6, which, as a legal document, was something I knew next to nothing about while I lived there. It was also on the Prairies where Idle No More was founded and took off in these same shopping malls and intersections that asserted living, breathing Indigenous culture into common spaces. Watching the footage of hundreds of bodies gathered to peacefully sing and drum in front of Edmonton's Canada Place where Jasper Avenue and 97 Street meet, I was completely overcome by the sight and possibility of change. I still feel a sense of home under those big skies, even if the dominant culture there alienates me to the point of isolation. It's also easily understood when I say I can never live there again. With each subsequent return, I am still reminded of feeling at once invisible and targeted from the moment I step off the plane. Whether the threat of whiteness is intentionally present or not, its reverberations are still inside me.

Concurrent with piecing together the history of my own lineage before arriving in this colony, I have been unlearning everything I absorbed about the official histories of Canada. After twenty years of access to a relatively excellent education system and a fairly democratic mass media, I started learning about the violence of this country's settler colonialism in 2008, when I first began seeing contemporary Indigenous artists representing their own stories and histories. I did not fully understand what took place inside residential schools until closer to 2012. I don't think I can ever fully understand, but I know I will never forget.

Growing up, I heard bits and pieces about Plains and Wood Cree, Nakota, Saulteaux, and Dene peoples, but mostly I had white friends and a couple of Métis and POC pals who didn't usually acknowledge their cultural backgrounds. I guess a lot of us didn't back then, for different reasons; under the logic of whiteness and colonization, we just found ways to drift toward each other. In another twenty years, what is going to happen when the majority of Canada's population shifts away from whiteness? Multiculturalism through the nation-state has been filtered through the state's level of tolerance. Being tolerated rather than accepted reveals the bedrock of prejudice beneath how the majority of Canadians still think about racial and cultural difference. We can only be different within a predetermined parameter of difference. If we stray too far from the tolerable behaviours of sharing our food and music and stories, often through designated times and spaces, then you are mocked if you are lighter-skinned like me, but if your skin is darker, and you say or do something unfamiliar, then I have seen the tension in the air shift toward you, and you are immediately under suspicion. I have seen on the streets, online, and in the news when you are attacked, arrested, and murdered because your difference becomes intolerable. I see you and affirm your experiences. I am sorry for not seeing you sooner.

PART III

As a former art critic, I have observed and written extensively on how this country sees itself through the art it makes and promotes regionally, nationally, and internationally. Canada may believe it is truly a progressive country, but its Indigenous, Black, and racially diverse artists exist only after they have exported themselves to international acclaim. This may be true on some level for all artists, writers, and musicians in Canada, who must find a larger market to survive before they are recognized at home, but when I look at the faces of tenured art professors, museum directors, senior curators, and almost every high-level executive position in the arts in this country, I see an overwhelmingly white landscape that prides itself on supporting diverse and Indigenous programming.

Some things are starting to change, and some things will stay the same.

Before I left Edmonton in the late 2000s, the first culturally diverse arts grants were being piloted on the municipal level. I was invited to sit on the jury, which was chaired by a white man with a white ponytail. It quickly became evident during our closed-door discussions that I had been asked to participate only because of my ethnic last name rather than my credentials as an art professional. But when I asked if I was eligible to apply for these culturally diverse grants, the answer was a head-shaking negative, as I was deemed "too Canadian" to qualify.

To be racialized is to be whatever's conveniently supporting the dominant narrative.

As I started travelling and working in different cities across the Prairies, and eventually across the country, the levels of racialization I experienced fluctuated, but its reality always remained. I never knew when or where this difference would be named, and how it was going to be used to categorize me, my intentions, my thoughts, wants, desires as somehow lesser than real.

Racial discrimination against Asian people is far less severe and fatal than the violent systematic prejudices against Black and Indigenous bodies. I'm not condoning the incessant microaggressions made against the middle-toned people on an everyday level, but I do believe in supporting the bigger picture. Specifically, Black and Indigenous voices have never been more resonant and visible in my lifetime than they are today, echoing past movements and momentums, and amplifying all who feel fed up and outraged at the ongoing abuses of white supremacy and the injustices of state policies and police brutality supported by and funded through the capitalist patriarchy of colonial law.

In Toronto specifically, I see strong bonds of allyship between current leaders of Indigenous resistance around the epidemic of missing and murdered Indigenous women and Black Lives Matter–TO. I will not speak on behalf of anybody from these movements, but only to what I have witnessed. I see young queer radical cis, trans, and non-binary folks at the forefront of these movements, and when I hear them speak about each other's actions and events, I hear a tremendous amount of support and care. From where I stand on the outside of these dynamics, I see a lot of respect between organizers, spreading awareness about each other's demonstrations through their online networks, and sharing resources like AV equipment and bodies in time and space. This holding up of each other in a city that may be diverse in appearance, but is still structurally white, is becoming the most unique characteristic about this place and, to some extent, about Canada itself. While for over 150 years, the structures of power have been shielding and protecting the settler-colonial dominance of entitled whiteness, what will happen in the future when whiteness is no longer the majority? I fear that settler entitlement will simply shift and those who have benefited directly from white imperialism will perpetuate this violence that spreads like a virus. Is the main difference between a settler and an immigrant the shape of each's entitlement? A settler arrives and brings with them a belief that what they "find" is theirs to keep and change, while an immigrant arrives and believes in learning and adapting to the laws and customs of their new homeland. Both require a certain sense of forgetting and belonging, and immigrants eventually become settlers under colonial mentality, but I want to imagine what would happen if every first-, second-, and third-generation Canadian stopped perpetuating colonial agendas, and instead supported Indigenous sovereignty by respectfully learning and obeying the original laws and customs on our adopted homelands. Specifically, I want to imagine the ever-displaced diasporas will stop pledging allegiance to a falling empire whose raiding history likely drove us away from our homelands in one way or another.

From its outset, as a colony in the fifteenth century, the land we now call Canada has been developed as a rich and stable country founded for its natural resources on the backs of Indigenous knowledge and labour, first in exporting fur and pelts to the near extinction of species, and now in its export of oil and gas and mineral extraction. The wealth generated from natural resource exports makes up a significant portion of Canada's GDP, and contributes to the high standard of living for most Canadians. So as we roll out land acknowledgements, are we also addressing the unjust and grossly disproportionate economic benefits derived from treaty and unceded land-based resources being siphoned off by the Crown? Just as Canada gained autonomy from Great Britain in 1931 and then finally severed its constitutional umbilical cord in 1982, will this country ever wean itself off its colonial roots by becoming an independent nation that honours its treaties through an Indigenous world view?

Today, Canada remains an extraction economy built in violation of Indigenous land rights and human rights. Successive generations of theft and broken promises to consult and respect Indigenous groups and decisions over land-based developments appear to salt the ongoing wound in Canadian and Indigenous relationships. The mere suggestion of land reform and repatriation angers and frightens many property owners new and old. For those few who have tried repatriating their land back to Indigenous nations, Canada's property laws remain a common obstacle. The country's economy will not crumble if Indigenous Nations were to take greater control over land-based resources, but this appears to be the underlying fear (and, for some, hope) that if we undo colonialism, we will undo capitalism.

I'm neither an anarchist nor a libertarian, but I do believe capitalism has long gone off the rails to the severe detriment of all living relationships. The dislocation of long-existing communities to increase production and profit includes a devastation of natural environments and patterns, an acceleration of climate change never before seen in human history, and a widening gap in income disparity and economic inequality. I am not proposing a complete overthrow of society as we know it, though I wouldn't entirely disagree with those who do. I do propose at some point in near futurity, Indigenous Nations who have lived and prospered on these territories for thousands of years be unequivocally accepted and recognized as the rightful keepers and stewards of the land and its resources. Then, and only then, will we truly be living in another time when all of us who have gathered here can acknowledge where we came from and how we collectively came to this point.

Acknowledgements

Thank you to the community organizers who have and continue to speak for those who can no longer be heard.

Deep gratitude to my co-publishers: Bopha Chhay from Artspeak for her tireless work on this manuscript and Jay and Hazel Millar from Book*hug for their enthusiastic support in taking this on and hitting the ground running.

Thank you to all the readers who deeply engaged. A multi-layered approach was taken to incorporate notes from general readers, sensitivity readers, and technical/structural/fact-checking readers for specific chapters as well as for the overall text throughout the course of the writing process. Listed here in no particular order, but with fondness and gratitude all the same, thank you: Kim Nguyen, Alex Leslie, Ariel Smith, Andrew Wilmot, Adriana Disman, Ted Kerr, Shawna Dempsey, Wanda Wilson, Megan MacKenzie, Divya Mehra, Janet Rogers, Indu Vashist, and Ayumi Goto for your generous feedback.

Sincere hands-together emojis to all the generous hosts who have made space and time for readings of chapters-in-progress over the past two years plus those who put me up, fed me, suggested and/ or loaned me books, drove me around, and assisted my research process in supportive, material ways. Thank you to: the Research Centre for Performance Art, Lesley Marshall, Sarah Patterson, Danielle Greer, Sarah Anne Johnson, Cecilia Berkovic, Kathy Ochoa, Yaniya Lee, Alexandra MacIntosh and Iris Stünzi (Shorefast Foundation), Lisa Baldissera and Joanne Bristol (Contemporary Calgary), Indu Vashist, Nahed Mansour and Toleen Touq (South Asian Visual Arts Centre), Michelle Schultz (dc3 Art Projects), Thea Bowering (Word/CJSR), Danielle St-Amour (Art Metropole), Kegan McFadden (Open Space), Davida Nemeroff (Night Gallery), Gelare

Khoshgozaran and Jimena Sarno, Niki Little and Becca Taylor (National Indigenous Media Arts Coalition), Matthew Hills and D'Arcy Wilson (Grenfell Art Gallery and Saltbox Arts Festival).

Additional thanks to Janet Rogers, Cecily Nicholson, Alex Leslie, and Eileen Myles for providing kind words at the end of this process.

I actually couldn't have done this without the support of my dear friends and loves that have put up with me and checked up on me over these past two years of transition.

And of course, thank you to my mother, for sharing her stories with me, and for everything else.

Reading List

This book does not exist in a vacuum.

Formative texts in my research process include Patricia Monture-Angus's *Thunder in My Soul: A Mohawk Woman Speaks*, Dionne Brand's *A Map to the Door of No Return*, Leanne Simpson's *This Accident of Being Lost*, Stuart Hall's *The Fateful Triangle*, and Arthur Manuel and Grand Chief Ron Derrickson's *Unsettling Canada: A National Wake-Up Call*. These works stayed with me longer than most.

Through the course of eighteen months of intense research and study, I want to acknowledge and thank the staff at the Vancouver City Archive, the City of Edmonton Archive, the Manitoba Archives, Bibliothèque et Archives nationales du Québec, the Toronto Reference Library, and the Parkdale branch of the Toronto Public Library.

I also want to make special mention of the incredible and generous resource of the University of Alberta's *Indigenous Worldviews* online course.

Other key reading materials include the *Royal Commission on Aboriginal Peoples* (1996), available on Library and Archives Canada, and *Honouring the Truth, Reconciling for the Future: Summary of the Final Report of the Truth and Reconciliation Commission of Canada* (2015).

All of these materials are available for free through most libraries and online.

Colophon

Manufactured as the first edition of *Before I Was a Critic I Was a Human Being* in the spring of 2019 by Book*hug Press and Artspeak

Copy edited by Stuart Ross
Type + design by Malcolm Sutton